WOUNDED HEART, HEALED SPIRIT

The Incredible True Story
of an Unlikely Follower of Jesus

CAROL CARLEY

WOUNDED HEART, HEALED SPIRIT
Copyright © 2023 by Carol Carley

Unless otherwise indicated, scripture quotations taken from the New English Bible, copyright © Cambridge University Press and Oxford University Press 1961, 1970. All rights reserved. Scripture quotations marked (NIV) taken from the Holy Bible, New International Version®, NIV®. Copyright © 1973, 1978, 1984, 2011 by Biblica, Inc.™ Used by permission of Zondervan. All rights reserved worldwide. www.zondervan.com The "NIV" and "New International Version" are trademarks registered in the United States Patent and Trademark Office by Biblica, Inc.™ Scripture quotations marked (NKJV) taken from the New King James Version®. Copyright © 1982 by Thomas Nelson. Used by permission. All rights reserved.

Soft cover ISBN: 978-1-4866-2472-0
Hard cover ISBN: 978-1-4866-2477-5
eBook ISBN: 978-1-4866-2473-7

Word Alive Press
119 De Baets Street Winnipeg, MB R2J 3R9
www.wordalivepress.ca

WORD ALIVE
—P R E S S—

Cataloguing in Publication information can be obtained from Library and Archives Canada.

*This book is dedicated to everyone
who has ever felt wounded,
with a prayer that the healing
they await will arrive soon.*

CONTENTS

INTRODUCTION

What happened to me at age twelve would forever leave an imprint on my life. Only when the undeniable power of God intervened years later did a welcome transformation begin. That's when I discovered that the journey I'd embarked on at that tender age had been marred by roadblocks and detours—and the choices I would make to overcome these obstacles would determine whether I was a victim or victorious.

Reflecting back upon this time decades later, it is clear that I was never alone, and that God was guiding every cautious step I took. He was the Master Weaver in the tapestry of my life. Only through the power of God's love, through answered prayer and some unanswered prayer, was I able to conquer the mountains that stood in my way.

As you acquaint yourself with my story, you may see glimpses of yourself and realize that we can choose to rise above the struggles that dare to crush us. By seeking, and discovering, a strength greater than our own, we can defeat these unwelcome circumstances. When we reach the crossroads in our journey, the point at which we find ourselves thanking God for the struggles, we will know that He has been at work in our lives.

Two major influences have shaped my life, neither of which I ever imagined would have such a momentous effect on my identity.

The first are my childhood memories, still vivid, of growing up in the shadow of a violent alcoholic father. Those early years crippled any sense of self-worth I might have hoped for. I was plagued by extreme shyness, unrelenting fear, and daunting hopelessness. I never felt like I really belonged anywhere. I believed my future had the same hope of taking flight as a deflated balloon.

Thus, my wounded heart.

The second influence has been my faith. When I realized that I was just as important to God as the other eight billion people on the planet, everything changed. I learned to surrender to God's guidance daily, allowing myself to feel His unconditional love anchoring me. I experienced the mystery and miracle of how God draws us closer to Himself, the unfathomable power of His grace and forgiveness, and the sustaining presence of His comfort and peace during sorrow and tragedy. God can use even an imperfect and unlikely follower of Jesus to bring glory to His name! He transformed my empty, fragmented life.

Thus, my healed spirit.

I take no joy or pleasure in revealing some of the sordid details I candidly share in this book, but I sincerely believe that alcoholism has destroyed countless lives and brought tragedy to far too many families. It is my hope that my transparency will inspire others who find themselves walking in these footsteps. Beyond loss, grief, and addiction, we can earnestly seek God with all our heart—and we will find Him.

That's not my promise. It's His.

Wherever you happen to find yourself on your journey today, my prayer is that my story will be a source of hope. Reach out, reach up, and claim victory in your life. You might be surprised at the tenacity and untapped courage within you, just waiting to be set free. After all, God is the Author of your story.

You may have already come face to face with challenges other than those which confronted me. But one certain truth remains: there is a power greater than our own. The way in which we acknowledge and embrace this power makes all the difference in how our pilgrimage begins. And ends.

You matter. Your life is precious and worthy of being celebrated! Many unique gifts within you are just waiting to be discovered, and some of those gifts may even be the struggles.

Even with all the fears, sorrow, and heartache that might wound you along the way, the journey is still worth taking. Your next step of faith may be the one that brings you that much closer to the bend in the road beyond which love, healing, and joy unspeakable await.

As sure as the sun will rise tomorrow, you are loved! You have dreams worth dreaming and mountains worth climbing. The God who has blessed you with both dreams and mountains beckons you now.

The next step is yours. Begin today. You will never be alone. Trust God. He will become your most faithful fellow traveller. With God as your guide, and the courage to follow, your life has never looked more promising!

CHAPTER ONE

TWELVE

My childhood memories still bring flashbacks from time to time. And although the gift of memory is one of God's greatest blessings, fleeting moments I have thought it to be a curse.

I was the second oldest of five children. Growing up in the quaint lakeside city of North Bay, Ontario, most of our neighbours knew each other on a first name basis. They were like an extended family and we had a real sense of community.

Many of the moms didn't work outside the home and baking was a favourite past-time. They felt free to knock on each other's doors to borrow a cup of sugar or an egg or two. The kids enjoyed popular outdoor games like hide and seek, kick the can, street hockey, hopscotch, and marbles. The innovative technologies of cell phones and the internet hadn't yet invaded.

For me, school offered a welcome reprieve from life at home. My teachers seemed genuinely considerate, cheerful, and attentive and I adored every one of them. It seemed the feelings were mutual, since my mom was told at many parent-teacher interviews that I was the teacher's pet. I loved staying after school to wipe off the blackboards, collect the chalk, and return abandoned books to their proper library shelves. These little chores helped delay whatever situation may have been waiting for me at home.

Besides overseeing their classes, my teachers made me feel special and treated me with kindness. That was just as important to me as learning the capital of Greenland or the significance of the prime meridian.

But the message I got from my dad was quite the opposite, so naturally the confusion about my self-worth grew. And the roots went deep.

I remember a particular history assignment. Like with all my schoolwork, I poured my heart and soul into the project, even researching related articles and pictures. When my teacher handed back my assignment, next to her flattering comments was my mark: ninety-eight percent. I had lost two points for lettering the pages alphabetically instead of numbering them. So much for trying to be different and colour outside the lines!

When I brought my project home to show my parents, my mom's eyes sparkled. Without her saying a word, I could tell she was beaming with pride. But when my dad glanced at my grade, all he managed to mutter was, "Not good enough." Those words planted the seed in my mind that nothing I did was ever good enough. To my twelve-year-old ears, it meant *I* wasn't good enough.

His insensitive comment left an emotional scar on my already shrinking self-image. I wondered if all fathers were that cruel to their children.

Years later, someone tried to tell me about God's love and I figured there was no point in even considering it. Since I hadn't been good enough for my own dad to love, there was no way for me to ever measure up to the unattainable expectations of God, my heavenly Father.

I couldn't have been more wrong. I hadn't yet learned that God's love was unconditional.

When I was at school, I did my best to conceal the fact that my dad was consumed by violence whether or not he consumed alcohol. My teachers showed me through their warm, caring attention and much-needed hugs that I was loveable. Isn't that all a child longs to know? That they're worthy enough to be loved?

If my teachers knew my dad was a drunk, I thought it would reflect back on me and they wouldn't like me anymore. I had convinced myself that it was at least partially my fault he got angry and drank, because I wasn't good enough. His drinking was my secret, and no matter how bad the verbal abuse got, I would never tell anyone.

But it was more of a challenge to hide the black and blue bruises, many of which resulted from my dad's out of control temper before he'd even touched a drop of his devil's brew.

Taking part in gym class was always a little tricky, especially in the girls' change room where we would put on our gym uniforms. I would make my way to a small, unoccupied corner. Sometimes I wouldn't get changed quickly enough and my classmates or teacher would notice the bruises and ask what had happened.

"I fell," I would answer, hoping the simple reply would satisfy their curiosity.

Sometimes when I was punished for something at home, my dad would whip me severely using the long black strap that hung in the pantry beside the kitchen. That strap was so thick and wide that it couldn't possibly have been used as a belt to hold up a man's pants; I concluded that it had probably been used to help control the animals on my grandpa's farm. I wondered if it was the same form of discipline my dad had experienced as a child. I have a feeling it bruised him before it bruised me.

I'm not sure what was more traumatic, being whipped with that leather strap so hard that stinging welts formed on my legs and bottom or realizing that a parent could do such a maniacal thing to a defenceless child. I think the latter. The bruises would eventually heal, but the memories still haven't.

When I wasn't at school, I devoted myself to taking care of my younger siblings. I also spent time helping my mom, my best friend. There were lots of household chores to do, including making meals, doing the laundry and hanging it on the clothesline, and ironing.

I often saw her come to the rescue of her innocent children, throwing herself in front of my dad's blistering hand or the strap that was intended for us. With my own eyes I witnessed my mom getting beaten up and worn down until there was just about no fight left in her. She was the first victim in a long line of people who endured physical scars at my dad's hands. I knew her self-worth couldn't plummet much further.

His frequent violent outbursts toward my mom became more explosive when he drank. However, the endless consumption of alcohol didn't only fuel his anger; he would also plough a path of destruction toward anything that got in his way, including furniture, family, or friends.

One night, I went to bed early after studying for an important test scheduled for school the next day. I was awakened by a loud crescendo of voices from the kitchen. I could hear my dad arguing with my two uncles, Ernie and Jimmy. All of them were drunk.

Just when I thought things couldn't get worse, I heard my dad yell my name from the bottom of the stairs.

Half-asleep, I walked to the landing and asked what he wanted. He demanded that I get downstairs immediately to wash the kitchen floor. I knew that an even worse fate awaited me if I refused.

With trepidation and fear, I walked down to the kitchen where I received my instructions to move the chairs out of the way, fill a bucket with hot, soapy water, and kneel with a cloth to wash the floor. When the humiliating task was done, I counted my blessings that I wasn't ordered to wash it a second time.

On those occasions when my mom had the strength, she would gather us kids and take us to stay with one of her close friends. I can only imagine how embarrassed she must have felt having to divulge the truth about my dad's drinking. She had spent years making excuses for him and covering everything up, just like we were learning to do. But sometimes we needed a safe, temporary shelter from the torment he unleashed. We might go for three or four nights at a time, always returning home before wearing out our welcome.

Thankfully, most of the nightmares about my childhood have greatly diminished. But the worst of my nightmares revolve around what would happen when it was time for bed. As children, we knew when we were upstairs that we were that much further removed from our defenceless mom downstairs. At night she was a sitting target. Her love for us children would anchor her feet to the living room floor like a brave warrior preparing for battle. She knew that if my dad was fighting with her, he wouldn't be fighting with us.

Instead of changing into our pyjamas, we three oldest children, used to the all too familiar nighttime routine, would huddle at the top of the stairs—sometimes for minutes, sometimes for hours. We'd be waiting to run downstairs to rescue our mom. We felt like a pack of lion cubs coming to the aid of their weak, vulnerable mother, easy prey for the deadly threats of a menacing intruder.

Sometimes we wouldn't make it downstairs soon enough. It was hard for us to accurately predict the eruption of hostility. When we didn't react in time, we would find our mom already lying on the floor or crouching behind a kitchen chair with her glasses knocked off or smashed. Other times her skin would be broken and we'd help clean up blood.

Scenes like these eroded our sense of normalcy, overshadowing our future lives and relationships as adults.

Between the echoes of our horror-filled cries, we usually managed to push our dad back into his living room chair, but we all knew that a beating like this might only be the first of many before the dawning of a new day. This senseless suffering often repeated itself throughout any given week.

I also have painful memories from my birthday celebrations. I never heard my dad wish me a happy birthday. I often wondered if he even knew the date of my birthday. Why wasn't it important enough for him to acknowledge?

One year, my mom wasn't as vigilant as usual. She baked me a chocolate cake and said I could invite a few school friends over. We both realized this was a huge risk, because we had no way of knowing whether my dad would be drunk that day.

Because my mom had planned the birthday gathering directly after school, and well before my dad arrived home from work, everything worked out. My friends and I celebrated precious moments together. We enjoyed games my mom had planned for us and indulged in homemade cake with ice cream.

Even though I felt blessed to have presents to open from my school friends, my memories of that birthday are better than any gift I could have unwrapped.

We were so poor that we never got to have second helpings of food at the dinner table, so I was pretty sure there was no extra money for birthday presents—not that I ever expected any. But one year I was thrilled to discover that my mom had wrapped some simple coins in wax paper and inserted them into my cake. What a wonderful surprise!

My dad's birthday had always presented a unique dilemma for me. Even well into my adult years, I could never find an appropriate card for him. The sentiments in the cards I saw at the store were typically filled with love, gratitude, respect, and warmest wishes to a deserving father for being so supportive. I couldn't relate. It often took me a long time to find the perfect card for my dad, and it usually just said a simple "Happy Birthday."

Without a doubt, the worst occasions, when his assaults hurt most of all, were Christmas. For our family, there was no silent night or peace on earth.

Although we would brace ourselves for what lay ahead, we did have a few moments of joy. Once December arrived, we'd look forward to the seasonal pilgrimage to our grandparents' farm. That was our invitation to pick the grandest Christmas tree we could find—and as soon as we brought it home, we would be excited to hang our homemade, heartfelt decorations on the branches, lit by the soft, mellow glow of strings of lights and crowned with a simple store-bought star.

Even so, we always knew such a magical moment of holiday cheer was temporary, that it would too soon fade. The view through our front living room window, if caught at just the right moment, might have resembled a Norman Rockwell painting, but ten minutes later it would be replaced with an image of my mom being thrown into the tree by our raging dad. This was an annual rite we came to expect and fear. It was just a matter of time.

How very badly we needed the Saviour of the season to transform our broken, fragile lives with the gifts of love, hope, and peace. But that wouldn't happen until many years later, after tragedy struck.

Although the birth of Jesus wasn't yet the focus of our humble Christmases, God would soon open a door for me—and give me the courage to somehow walk through it.

On a typical weeknight, instead of doing homework at the kitchen table I was allowed to invite Valerie, a school friend, to our house to work on a special project together. While we were upstairs, the intensity of my dad's shouting and swearing became deafening. I suggested to Valerie that she better go home, either because of my own embarrassment or fear over how the script would inevitably end. It probably was both.

I walked with Valerie to the front door, said goodnight, and had just turned to go back upstairs when there was a knock at the door. It was Valerie again, standing in the shadow of nightfall. I didn't see any angelic wings, but with a gentle voice and compassionate heart she said, "Carol, you're not staying here tonight. You're coming home with me."

After telling my mom that Valerie had invited me to spend the night at her house, I gathered a few simple belongings into my little blue suitcase and kissed and hugged my mom goodnight.

That was bittersweet. I felt fortunate enough to have a safe haven, but I was worried about my mom. The only consolation, the only thing that convinced me to leave with Valerie, was that my thirteen-year-old brother David was home. I knew he would be a valiant adversary against the Goliath-like monster plotting his next attack from the living room.

When I closed the door behind me that night, I had no way of knowing that God was about to alter my circumstances. Looking back at His handiwork, I can see how He was opening doors while closing a few others. My incredible journey of faith as an unlikely follower of Jesus was only just beginning.

CHAPTER TWO

ON MY OWN

Staying at Valerie's house was a godsend, but I knew it wouldn't last forever. Her single mom was a nurse and I didn't want to be an added hardship for them. Their plans didn't include caring for the needs of an extra house guest.

But the several nights I spent under their roof gave me enough time to figure out my options.

Instead of returning home, I decided that I needed to find the courage to share my predicament with Shelley, a friend in my Grade Eight class. I thought she might have some idea of where I could find a place to live.

Unknown to me at the time, she had already asked her parents if I could stay with their family for a while.

They did, in fact, invite me to move in. I was incredibly thankful, especially since Shelley had lots of brothers and sisters, meaning there were already a lot of mouths to feed. I couldn't help feeling a little guilty knowing they had to stretch their grocery budget to make ends meet. But Shelley's parents never made me feel like a burden. Quite the opposite. They were thoughtful and caring, and they lived by the golden rule.

After living with Shelley and her family for a couple of months, a window of opportunity presented itself. More accurately, it was one of those many doors God has opened throughout my life.

Valerie's mom was friends with a nurse who was going back to work after her maternity leave. This nurse, Carol Ann, needed a full-time babysitter. She got in touch with me and we soon met. After a successful interview and getting acquainted with Kevin, her adorable blond-haired, blue-eyed six-month-old son, there I was—Mary Poppins in training!

As a bonus, Carol Ann had a permanent nightshift working from 11:30 p.m. until 8:00 a.m. and needed someone who was able to sleep over. We came to an amicable agreement. Under the circumstances, the obvious solution was for me to live with them. It was an answer to prayer, for both of us. My fear of becoming homeless was postponed and it was time to pack my suitcase again.

Throughout the following years, I kept in close contact with my mom and even dropped in to see her several times a week when I was sure my dad wasn't home. She told me that my brother David had quit school and taken a job with the railroad up north. I especially missed seeing him but realized he had goals of his own to pursue.

I was also pleased to learn that my dad had stopped drinking and secured a full-time job. But his violent behaviour had persisted.

One afternoon when my high school classes finished early, I had coffee with my mom and enjoyed some of her home baking. I spread my homework out on the kitchen table as we chatted, making progress with my assignments. We both treasured our heart-to-heart talks.

Suddenly we heard a car pull into the driveway. To our surprise, my dad had come home early from work. I hadn't seen or talked to him for a couple of years. Knowing he was only a few steps away paralyzed me with fear. My heart pounded in my chest as panic set in.

I gathered all my schoolwork and hugged my mom goodbye as she hurried to wash our coffee mugs. When my dad walked in the front door, I was already silently exiting the house through the trap door in the pantry. I found my footing on the old wooden ladder which led to the basement and quietly closed the door.

Behind me, I heard my dad walk down the front hallway and into the living room. I pried open a basement window, climbed out, and ran to the back yard. All I had to do next was climb over the fence into the overgrown laneway. Once I made it that far, I was home free.

Not too long after that, I had another close encounter. I happened to be strolling along our town's main street when I looked ahead and noticed the unmistakable figure of my dad about a block away. He was walking on the same side of the street as me, coming in my direction.

My heart raced, breaking its natural rhythm, and I could feel it pulsating in my throat. I just knew everyone around me could hear it. How could I avoid coming face to face with my dad? This time there was no convenient trap door nearby.

Within minutes, we were passing one another, practically in each other's shadow. I thought to myself that he might say hi or ask how I'd been doing. Better still, maybe he'd stop, hug me, and say how good it was to see me… and how sorry he was for everything that had ever happened when he was drinking.

But none of the above took place. We simply passed each other on the street. He didn't even know it was me. Although the same blood ran through our veins, we were like complete strangers— two lost, hurting souls whose differences kept us worlds apart.

We didn't see each other again for a couple of years. I wanted us to reconcile as best we could, though, so I worked toward establishing a tolerable relationship with him.

Even though I wasn't faced with his daily confrontations, though, the lingering effects of having grown up in such an unhealthy home still manifested. This became clear in many ways.

I was crippled by extreme shyness, a symptom of my lack of self-worth. If I was walking in the old neighbourhood and noticed someone coming toward me, I would cross the street as we got closer. I thought I was ugly, worthless, and of no value to anyone. In the few seconds it took to pass someone on the street, I would imagine them secretly making all kinds of judgments about me—how I looked, the clothes I was wearing, if I was pretty or not, and basically whether I deserved to be taking up space on the sidewalk. Or the planet.

With such a crushing self-image, it's no wonder I created barriers around me and built walls like a mighty fortress.

Having so few people to share my deepest feelings with, I started pouring my thoughts down on paper. Even though it was a painful exercise, seeing the words take shape seemed to affirm the reality of my journey.

Eventually, writing became a deep joy for me. Reading my poems and songs validated who I was. It became comforting and cathartic.

Throughout high school, I was fortunate to have several teachers I absolutely adored. Next to my mom, my favourite person was an English teacher who nurtured my love of writing so much that it helped me develop some self-esteem. He was a constant source of encouragement and I was incredibly humbled when he told me to keep writing because, as he said, I had "a gift."

But truly, he was the gift. He was a huge positive influence on my life, then and now. In fact, with his guidance and support I summoned enough courage to share some of my songs. I had several opportunities over the years to sing, including at school assemblies, hootenannies, concerts, and special local events. Both of my younger sisters sang too, and one of them played guitar.

Something wonderful happened after my sisters and I sang one evening at a popular coffee house in town. That night, a television producer just happened to be in the audience. After the performance he approached and invited us to be guests on an upcoming variety show.

I was ecstatic! After all those years of hiding my feelings, here was someone who thought my songs were good enough to be heard on the public airwaves. Things were looking up!

They were about to get even more intriguing. On the night we were scheduled to sing on TV, several classmates told me they would be watching. This included Ian, a friend of mine.

After the show, one of Ian's best friends, John, told him that he really wanted to meet me. But I had more important things to do, like get ready for my graduation. I had managed to put myself through high school and even filled out the college applications to enroll in a journalism program. I knew I would need to apply for a student loan, but I had received a scholarship that would lighten the financial load.

I also had to explain to Carol Ann that I intended to move three hundred miles away to attend college in Kitchener.

In any event, I had no time to drop everything just to meet one of Ian's friends, someone I would probably never cross paths with again. That's why it was pointless to start a friendship with some guy named John Carley.

CHAPTER THREE

ACQUAINTED WITH GRIEF

L ittle did I know that God was in control. I soon met John Carley—and married him. But that's another story.

A few years after graduating from college, John and I made our home in Kitchener-Waterloo where I started a career in public relations. Meanwhile John pursued a combined master's degree in social work and divinity.

Before getting married, we had thought it would be important and meaningful to start attending the church where we intended to exchange our wedding vows. Before long, we were celebrating our first anniversary and life seemed full. We made friends in the congregation, became youth group leaders, and started a monthly evening program called Faith, Films, and Fellowship. I also sang in the choir and John became the beloved church ordinand.

Life was bliss. Until it wasn't.

No one runs to answer a phone with great excitement at three o'clock in the morning, but one night, awakened from his sleep, John hesitantly got up to answer it.

When he picked up the receiver, he heard my dad's voice. Nothing could have prepared us for the conversation that followed.

My brother David, twenty-six, had died in a car accident. He had worked many years for the railroad and had been driving home from northern Ontario for Thanksgiving. Two co-workers had been with him, both asleep in the back seat. Exhausted from work and the long drive, David had fallen asleep at the wheel and his car went over an embankment. He died in the ambulance en route to the hospital.

I was told that both of his co-workers walked away without so much as a scratch.

John and I headed home, but not for the Thanksgiving weekend we had envisioned. There was much silence between us during the five-hour drive to North Bay. The grief was too great for words. We had been looking forward to Thanksgiving and planning to spend time with family and renew our ties with old friends. Instead we were getting together to choose hymns and scriptures for my brother's funeral.

The chapel overflowed with David's friends. It was standing room only, a true testament to the many lives my brother had touched. In all directions, we could see nothing but an infinite array of flowers beckoning from every side of the room. Their vibrant colours and heavenly scent almost made us think we were there to celebrate a happier occasion—that is, until the minister started speaking. His sombre words, magnified by the sting of death, pierced our souls.

Our return trip home wasn't any easier, and soon I would be back in the familiar routine. I'd be going to work and John would be continuing his classes.

I remember my first day back at the office. My co-workers were considerate and gave me the space I needed to get back into work mode.

But one conversation, a sorry attempt at compassion, still stands out in my mind. More than forty years after losing my brother, one memory still evokes anger from time to time.

A colleague stopped by my office to see me—to offer her condolences, I think. During our conversation she asked if David had been married.

"No," I replied.

"And did he have any children?"

"No."

"Oh, he was lucky."

Speechless, every fibre of my being tensed up. I wasn't sure how to respond. I didn't appreciate this flippant comment. "Lucky" isn't the word that came to mind after just returning from my brother's funeral.

Having reflected on her words for years, I'm sure she meant well. She was trying to be sincere, but that wasn't the message I needed to hear at that stage of my loss.

Ever since that poignant moment, I make sure, when offering my sentiments of comfort to those who mourn, to choose my words wisely. Grief can remain raw for a very long time. It's better to sit silently with a friend in their sorrow than to wound them with insensitive comments, intentional or not. In times of loss, people aren't looking for theological platitudes or worn-out cliches. They do need our presence, and even good old-fashioned hugs.

The gift of our time is often the only act of kindness needed to bring hope to a hurting heart. Just sitting in silence can be enough to say that we love someone and care. No words needed.

FOR THE LOVE OF DAVID[1]

He was just a carefree spirit with the wind
blown through his hair
and he lived his life as full as he could live.
He didn't have a lot of money, but he didn't really care,
'cause he was rich in love and gave all he could give.
And the railroad was his passion;
he had worked there many years,
telling stories of the places he would go.
And my heart still fills with gladness
though my eyes swell up with tears
every time I hear that old train whistle blow.

<u>Chorus</u>
For the love of David and brothers everywhere,
for all the loved ones we've lost along the way.
How we'll cherish all the good times and the memories we share;
we still think of you with fondness every day.
For the love of David and the many lives you touched,
for all the loved ones our hearts have to let go.
Never knew that loving you and losing you could hurt so much,
but in your heart I hope you'll always know I love you so.

You probably know that you're an uncle now;
we've had a family too
and so many things have changed since you've been gone.
I still look at all your pictures and the photographs of you;
sometimes they give me strength to carry on.
And if only I could phone you to talk with you a while,
that would really be long distance where you are.

---

[1] This is a song I wrote about my brother, many years after he died.

But maybe heaven's so much closer, we can't measure it in miles;
I feel you near me so it can't be very far.

(Chorus)

I find myself still asking questions of why you had to go,
and there's an emptiness inside I can't explain.
Yet I sense you all around me and I just wanted you to know
I'll try to be real strong until we meet again.
I guess God in all His wisdom needed you with Him;
who else could make the angels laugh or sing so sweet?
And I believe with all my heart that together
we'll both laugh again
and it will be a great reunion when we meet.

(Chorus)

CHAPTER FOUR

STANDING IN HEAVEN

My life continued to be busy with the demands of work and becoming more involved at church. We seemed to spend extra time mentoring the teenagers in our youth group, with whom we had built deep relationships.

After the loss of David, though, the broken-hearted days turned into broken-hearted weeks. I tried to portray a strong sense of fortitude in front of others, but two penetrating questions kept tugging at my soul: had David known I loved him, and was he in heaven with God?

Even though I had gone to church since age five, I wasn't sure where to find the answers.

My involvement with the church choir and my passion for music anchored my feet to the choir loft floor in my youth. I wouldn't really seek a closer relationship with God until I was in my mid-twenties. But I still had some hope within me that if I turned to Him for answers, He would hear me.

One night, I had a divine encounter that became the foundation in my journey to seek, know, love, and serve Him. I wanted to unabashedly shout from the mountaintop, "God is alive and He loves you!"

Before going to sleep, I felt compelled, almost directed, to kneel on the floor beside my bed and pour out my heart to God. I grabbed my pillow and held it to my face, sobbing so much that it was barely dry. I felt like I was drowning in my tears and wasn't yet able to say anything; the agony of loss was unbearable. But I knew the only way out of the pain was to go through it.

Suddenly, the fragmented words of my first serious prayer broke through the darkness: "God, I need to know David is all right. I need to know he's with You. I need to know he's in heaven. And I need to know *tonight*."

Exhausted from my pleading, I picked myself up off the floor and literally fell into bed.

Sometime during the night, I awakened to find myself standing in a beautiful meadow. It seemed like the closest place to paradise I had ever been. Everything around me was in living technicolour, not the regular sort of colours I was familiar with.

A babbling brook ran just to my right, cascading over rocks. The sound of lapping water seemed to praise God. So did the wind in the trees! The flowers looked like velvet as they swayed gently in the breeze, and even this slight movement magnified God. The sun's rays beckoned, also glorifying God. Everything in God's heavenly creation, everything His hands had fashioned, was worshipping its Maker!

Hearing this symphony of sound reminded me of the lyrics to the famous Christmas carol: "And heaven and nature sing…"

I don't know how long I stood listening to heaven sing its praises; it was timeless. But I soon became focused on the faint image of an approaching figure in the distance. Was someone coming towards me?

After a few seconds, I recognized it as my brother, David. There was no doubt about it. He was wearing his blue jeans and red plaid railroad shirt.

Soon he was standing right in front of me with a radiant smile on his face. He began communicating silently. There was no need to speak aloud because we could clearly read each other's thoughts. He simply thought what he wanted to say, and I heard it.

As I intently looked into his eyes, he said, "Carol, look where I am." He outstretched his arms, taking in everything around him. David continued to convey his thoughts and I understood what he said: "Go back and tell Mom and Dad that I'm here. I'm fine."

Once David had given me this message, a magnetic force seemed to slowly pull him back away from me. He eventually faded into the distance and I couldn't see him anymore.

Then I felt the sensation of being pulled back too… and a moment later, I found myself sitting up in bed. Could it have been a dream? Maybe.

But did I believe it had been a dream? Not in a million years! Somehow, and I can't even venture a guess as to how, I knew that I had been standing in heaven. God, rich in compassion and love, had transported me to see David. I had witnessed with my own eyes that my brother was very much alive—well, happy. And I had been given a hopeful message from him to relay to our parents.

When I got up from bed the next morning, my heart was light. A heavy burden had been lifted. I kept reliving my heavenly experience, of crying out to God and being heard, of having my desperate prayer answered that same night. Unlimited by time or space, or anything else, God had made a way for me to see my brother again.

That day, I phoned my mom to tell her what had happened and pass on David's message. I believe that was the day her heart began its lengthy recovery toward healing, hope, comfort, and peace.

As I reflect today on those moments of experiencing heaven, I feel blessed to realize that this is where my belief in miracles began. With that rare glimpse of such a celestial place, I was able to experience the true meaning of harmony. Everything in God's creation had been perfect in every detail, content and alive with wonder! And so had David.

CHAPTER FIVE
FIRST STEPS

Through John's studies at seminary, we became very close friends with a young couple named Mark and Patty. Mark was also a candidate for ministry. We got together at every opportunity, whether at our place or driving to see them in Harriston, a little town about an hour away. We usually visited them on Sunday and then after dinner attended the evening service where Mark served as student pastor.

Mark and Patty were passionate Christians and their faith glowed from the inside out. They shared their faith from time to time but never pressured us. I'm sure they must have been praying that we would discover a closer relationship with God.

One day they excitedly shared about a special event taking place at Wilfrid Laurier University in Waterloo. The pastor who oversaw Mark's studies, Gord, was the featured guest speaker. In addition, there would be uplifting Christian music from a dynamic worship band.

John and I gladly decided to attend. We had met Pastor Gord on previous occasions in Harriston.

As Friday night approached, I reflected on my journey of faith and what I hoped to take away from the event. My faith journey had only just begun. Oh, I had sung in the junior church choir at age five before graduating to the intermediate and senior choirs.

But that didn't take any faith on my part. I had loved singing and the choir had merely fulfilled one of my needs.

Now in my mid-twenties, I was co-leading the church youth group with John. This was about building meaningful relationships and giving the young adults a safe place to explore their questions about God and make sure they had lots of fun in the process.

Then it dawned on me that I'd previously made two important decisions that *had* required some amount of faith. The first was when I'd run away from home believing that I could conquer the future. The second was the night I had fallen on my knees at my bedside and reached out to a God I hoped was real and could answer my prayer.

As I remembered the strength and courage—and yes, even faith—it had required for me to make these life-changing decisions, I took my seat at the conference. I hoped to find deeper answers about God and better understand what my faith had to do with Him. There seemed to be a deep longing in my heart to find and know Him. And I didn't even realize at the time, but He was the One who had so masterfully nurtured that seeking within me. It was like a seed had been sown that needed to be cultivated and watered in order for it to grow and bear fruit.

All I knew when I walked into that university conference room was that my heart seemed filled with emptiness, a sadness void of any purpose. It was a burden to carry. How could I have possibly known God was about to wipe away every tear, transform my sadness into great joy, and see my heart reborn? Through my faithful trust in Him, God would use this moment of surrender to show me that He was the only Father I ever needed. He was the Father of a lifetime, unconditionally loving me as His daughter not because of who I was but because of who He was.

The conference started. The singing began. And that was music to my ears!

CHAPTER SIX

JUST AS I AM

It was amazing to stand and sing with hundreds of people, joining our hearts and voices together. But this wasn't just singing. We were united by a common purpose to offer our deepest praise and heartfelt worship to God.

As melodies of old, familiar hymns, and contemporary choruses echoed through the halls, there was an electricity in the air I had never felt or witnessed before. Everyone seemed filled with genuine anticipation of what the night would bring.

I was happy to comfortably stay in my seat and fade into the crowd, plagued by shyness and an innate lack of self-worth. I truly felt relieved to go unnoticed.

After the opening praise and worship ended, it was time for Pastor Gord to offer his message. John and I felt fortunate to have heard him speak before and agreed that he was gifted in sharing the Gospel. He could deliver a simple biblical message, but there always seemed to be a power transcending his words. I was riveted to every word he spoke. I'm sure he had given that sermon countless times, but it was the first time I really grasped that Jesus loved me enough to die for me.

While he ministered, a veil was lifted from my eyes. I understood that even I could experience the good news of salvation. I didn't have to feel like a failure because of my dad's words. I *was* good enough. I had to find the strength within me to let those wretched words die. It was clear that I needed to take a step of faith to quench the fear that imprisoned me in my own mind.

When Pastor Gord gave an invitation for people to come forward, the crowd prayerfully rose to their feet. It was like a heavenly chorus of angels, the singing seeming to transform into sacred worship. People of all ages made their way to receive prayer, forming a long line across the front of the room. Pastor Gord waited on the far left. There were so many people that I wondered how even one more person could possibly squeeze into the line.

The worship team started singing that anointed hymn "Just as I Am." I had sung those words before, but that night they brought a conviction to my spirit that God would accept me just as I was, even though I was imperfect, afraid, and a broken vessel. I trusted that I was good enough for Him.

Then I joined my voice with the others as we sang: "Just as I am, though tossed about with many a conflict, many a doubt, fightings and fears within, without, O Lamb of God, I come, I come."[2]

No truer words could ever have been written about my life and where I stood at the crossroads. Though the hymn was written in 1835, at the conference that Friday night on April 27, 1979, I felt like those lyrics by Charlotte Elliot had been written just for me.

Undaunted, I moved out of my comfort zone and approached the front of the room. Standing in the centre, I couldn't see the beginning of the prayer line. Or the end.

While I waited for Pastor Gord, I decided to put my time to good use. I bowed my head and began to pray aloud. No one could hear me, but that didn't matter; I knew this was my moment, a divine appointment with God I had anticipated for a long time.

---

[2] Charlotte Elliott, "Just as I Am," 1835.

The worship music continued and I sensed many people were being prayed for by friends as well as the prayer team. I felt incredibly humbled just to stand there, one among so many others who had worthy needs of their own. My prayer was spontaneous and unrehearsed, nothing like the refined, fluent prayers sometimes printed in store-bought greeting cards. I was simply surrendering to God and conveying how much I needed Him in my life.

I remember exactly what I said, like it was yesterday.

"God, I have given You twenty percent, sixty percent, eighty percent, and even ninety-nine percent of my life, but tonight I am trusting You one hundred percent to come into my life."

CHAPTER SEVEN

BLINDED BY THE LIGHT

As I stood there, I watched Pastor Gord approach until he was standing right in front of me. When our eyes met, I welcomed his warm and reassuring smile. He had given the invitation to anyone who wanted to receive Jesus, so we both knew why I was there.

He reached out, gently placed both of his hands on my head, and said, "Carol, repeat after me: Jesus…"

"Jesus," I said.

But before I had a chance to repeat the rest of the prayer, something totally unexpected and incredible happened. From the top of my head through every inch of my body, power surged. I can only compare it to what billions of volts of lightning must feel like. It wasn't scary. It didn't hurt. It was just waves of energy, washing over me so powerfully that I couldn't remain standing.

Before I knew it, I was on the floor. Later I found out that Mark had been standing behind me and gently placed me there. I was so thankful that the conference continued on with all the singing, prayer, and worship; the last thing I would have wanted was to create a scene or be the centre of attention. Hundreds of people moved around, not even noticing me. I felt relieved.

While I lay there with my eyes closed, I perceived a blinding light, dazzling and shimmering like diamonds. The brightest stars in the darkest night are dull and pale compared to that light I witnessed. And I knew only one light could outshine all the radiance of the universe: the Light of the World.

That's when I realized I was looking at Jesus, whose name I had just called upon. He didn't wear a robe or have sandals like we may expect. He was pure light. Even now, I fail to find the words to aptly portray its magnitude. The moment was indescribable.

He didn't speak. He didn't have to. His only purpose was to show me that when I opened the door, He would come in.

> Here I stand knocking at the door; if anyone hears
> my voice and opens the door, I will come in…
> (Revelation 3:20)

An even greater revelation was about to take place. As I continued to lie on the floor, basking in the Light of the Son, my stomach churned. All I could think of was that I had just accepted Jesus as my Lord and Saviour. Was I now going to be sick?

The churning sensation continued from the depths of my stomach. Then I felt it move all the way up my throat. As I opened my mouth, I heard myself speaking in a heavenly language:

> As Scripture says, "Streams of living water shall
> flow out from within him." He was speaking of
> the Spirit which believers in him would receive
> later; for the Spirit had not yet been given, because
> Jesus had not yet been glorified. (John 7:39)

I had only accepted Jesus moments earlier, so I had no idea what was happening.

Mark, who had been kneeling nearby, then handed me a piece of paper with something written on it. I learned later that I had been speaking in a foreign language and God had given Mark the gift of interpretation.

> In each of us the Spirit is manifested in one particular way, for some useful purpose… yet another has the gift of ecstatic utterance of different kinds, and another the ability to interpret it. But all these gifts are the work of one and the same Spirit, distributing them separately to each individual at will. (1 Corinthians 12:7, 10–11)

Here are the words of interpretation that Mark wrote on that paper:

> My daughter, I am so pleased with your trust in Me. As you remain faithful to Me, I will guide and direct your life and you and your husband will minister to your family, to all My people, to the glory of God the Father.

That piece of paper has been tucked inside my Bible for more than forty-five years. Although the ink has slightly faded, the power of that message has only been magnified.

That was the one and only time I ever spoke in tongues. But its influence on my faith has been enough for a lifetime.

I had gone to hear a Christian speaker, a pastor friend, with the hope of getting some answers for this new journey I was embarking on. But when John and I left the university that night, I only had more questions. So many questions.

I hadn't sought this experience. I certainly hadn't forwarded a specific request to God for me to speak in tongues. How could I have? I wasn't too familiar with my Bible and was unaware of the topic. I didn't know it was even possible this side of heaven.

Afterward, as I studied the Bible more, especially anything to do with the Holy Spirit and the variety of gifts He dispenses, I became hungry to learn as much as I could. My search for the truth became an even greater priority.

When we befriended Mark and Patty, we met many other members of their family, including Lynn, Mark's sister. She was very open in sharing her faith and prayer life. She had always felt it was essential to know what the scriptures taught. I'd say that one of the most important lessons I learned from Lynn was to commit to prayer any question I had in my Christian walk. If I didn't understand something, I should ask God to confirm whether it was true. If something was founded on biblical truth, Lynn assured me, it would be confirmed most often through scripture, although there were other ways too.

That sounded like wise advice. It's a practice I have continued for all these years. The process has never failed me.

With everything that happened at the conference, I decided that I needed time to reflect and put it all in perspective. I planned to delve into the scriptures and glean some answers. I knew one thing for sure: no one could ever accuse my Bible of needing to be dusted off.

CHAPTER EIGHT
HE TOUCHED ME

The following morning seemed to arrive earlier than usual, and John suggested that we treat ourselves to breakfast at a quaint coffee shop near our home. After that, we needed to buy groceries, finish the housework, and do laundry. It was back to the regular routine of daily life.

We no sooner got home when Mark and Patty phoned to invite us for Sunday dinner at their place. Then we could all attend the evening service together. It sounded like a wonderful idea and we were delighted to visit their warm, welcoming country church again.

Patty was like Martha Stewart in the kitchen, so we certainly felt pampered as guests at their dining room table. Our conversations with them were always easy-going and we appreciated their great sense of humour.

After we all pitched in to get the dishes done, we headed to church. It would be immensely meaningful for me to see Pastor Gord again, now that I'd committed my life to Christ two nights before.

Upon arriving, Mark and Patty soon got busy greeting parishioners. We decided to seat ourselves in the second last pew in the middle. I sat immediately next to the centre aisle, with John on my right. This may seem like an insignificant detail, but it's paramount to how the service unfolded.

Mark walked to the front and formally welcomed everyone. Then we joined our voices together in some favourite songs, the lyrics of which were all typed and fastened into a simple duotang booklet.

After the congregational singing, Lynn, who oversaw the music, went to the front and introduced two girls, about age ten, who had been invited to sing. As they sang about friendship, their angelic voices and youthful innocence spoke to me. I felt blessed to have such dear friends not only at our home church in Kitchener but also here in Harriston.

While the charming duet continued, I bowed my head to pray. Tears rolled down my cheeks and I tried not to move or draw attention to myself. I didn't pray aloud; it was a silent prayer of thanksgiving. I thanked God for blessing John and me with such close friends in two different congregations. With my head bowed and my eyes closed, I felt humbled to believe He loved us enough to direct our path toward such faithful Christian friends, mentors, and pastors.

I quietly wiped my face and started to gain more control over my emotions. Then I felt whoever was sitting behind me place their hand firmly on my left shoulder and keep it there for about ten seconds. This person had obviously noticed that I found the song especially meaningful and was reaching out to comfort me.

Soon after, the congregation stood to sing a hymn. This felt like an appropriate time to thank the thoughtful person who had reached out to console me—but when I turned around to offer my thanks, no one was there. The pew was empty.

I made sure to look from that aisle seat all the way around to the far right. To my amazement, not one person sat in that pew. I was baffled.

As the congregation sat down to listen to Mark's sermon, I don't recall hearing a word of it. All I could think about was what had just happened moments earlier. Had I imagined the whole thing?

Throughout the sermon, I silently prayed to God, asking if He had been the one to put His hand on my shoulder. And just as Lynn had taught me, I told God that if He confirmed it, I would believe it.

The whole experience seemed surreal. In that moment, I thought there was a good chance I was losing my mind. Yet, remembering what had happened two nights earlier when I'd invited Jesus into my heart, why should I have been so surprised?

Since I'd started going to church at age five, I could often recall ministers saying, "With God, all things are possible." And as a young child, my mom had often told me, "God works in mysterious ways, His wonders to perform." And I couldn't forget a favourite saying of mine: "Miracles happen to those who believe in them."

All this contemplation about the nature of God reminded me of another scripture:

> "Things beyond our seeing, things beyond our hearing, things beyond our imagining, all prepared by God for those who love him", these it is that God has revealed to us through the Spirit. (1 Corinthians 2:9–10)

I had only been a Christian for two days, and I could freely admit to having a simple, childlike faith. It would take a while to reach the point of putting my complete trust in God. But I knew I couldn't do it partway; it was all or nothing.

My faith is based on trusting that God, in all His wisdom, knows best how to reach us. At times it's a mystery. He is in control. The script is His. And if we dare to believe, we can know the purpose He has designed for us. God is the director and we are part of His plan, not the other way around.

With the service coming to an end, I looked at my printed bulletin and realized there was only the closing hymn left to sing before everyone met in the fellowship hall downstairs for refreshments. I silently wondered when, how, or even if God would confirm whether He had placed His hand on my shoulder to comfort me. Had I been hallucinating?

Lynn, sitting at the front, then stood up and walked forward. She turned around to face the congregation and said, "We aren't going to be singing the closing hymn printed in your bulletin. Instead please turn to the front page of your music booklet to the song 'He Touched Me.'"

Talk about a confirmation from the Lord! I was speechless. My mouth was dry and my heart was beating so loud that I could hear it pounding in my throat. I could barely stand.

John, as well as the rest of the congregation, was completely oblivious as to what had been happening to me since I'd walked through the church's front door.

The smell of freshly brewed coffee was now permeating every corner of the church and within minutes the congregation made their way downstairs. But before John followed, I told him that I needed to sit down for a moment.

I sat there, feeling numb and a bit shaken, and stared at the front of the church. I didn't know what to think. I had gone to church my whole life and probably listened to thousands of sermons, but none of that could explain the phenomenal experiences of the past two and a half days. God hadn't revealed Himself to me in a church; it had happened in a university hall. An ordained minister hadn't taught me about Jesus; my friends had.

I'd had an undeniable encounter with the living God through His Son, Jesus Christ, the Light of the World. I didn't need to wait until I died and went to heaven to meet Jesus. I had met Him face to face through a vision He'd given me. I simply had to call upon His name.

I watched the candles cast their shimmering glow, unable to feel their warmth from where I was seated in the second last pew. But I knew they were shedding light on everything around them. Maybe someday, I thought, I could be like a candle—on fire for God, shining for Jesus, bringing warmth and light to everyone who needed it.

As I quietly reflected on recent events, I asked Him to help me remain open to anything He brought my way. If He confirmed it, I would believe it.

Then I began to contemplate what the next part of my journey would be. I prayed that God would bless me with the courage and conviction to spread His love and His Word to others.

I'm not sure how much time passed, but I eventually decided it would be prudent to make an appearance downstairs. As I stood and turned around, though, I noticed a figure standing to my left at the back of the church.

Slowly but deliberately, I walked towards this person. They were wearing a white, hooded cloak that overflowed onto the floor. I presumed it was a woman. If she had been standing there for much of the church service, I'm sure she would have noticed who was sitting behind me. Maybe she could help clear up the mystery of who had put their hand on my shoulder. My intention was to find whoever it was and thank them.

By this time, I was only a couple of steps away from her. She stood motionless. I couldn't see her hair because of the hood shrouding her face, but I did notice her kind, gentle eyes.

Looking straight at her, I began to explain what I'd felt when those two little girls had started singing the song about friendship.

At that point, I remember asking my heart-burning question: "Do you know who it was?"

I waited intently for her answer and thought we would have a conversation about it, regardless of how long or brief it was. But instead, without moving or wavering, she spoke just three words to me: "The Holy Spirit." To this day, I still find her succinct response quite curious.

I glanced back at the pew where I'd sat, reliving the experience in my mind.

When I turned back to continue talking to the woman, she was gone. She was nowhere to be found. I hadn't heard her footsteps leaving or the sound of the heavy church door opening or closing.

I can't say for certain who she was. The only conclusion that makes any sense at all is that she was an angel, sent to deliver a message.

By now you've probably guessed that I never made it downstairs for coffee. As we left, John and I said our goodbyes and hugged Mark and Patty.

On our drive home, I had a lot to think about. Most of all, I kept wondering how an unlikely follower of Jesus, like me, could have such an extraordinary walk with God.

ALONG THE WAY[3]

Along the way, will You show me things
that You would have me do?
Along the way, help me live a life that's pleasing, Lord, to You.
Give me faith that I will follow in the footsteps where You lead.
Use my life to make a difference when I see someone in need.
Along the way, shine Your light in me so others will see You.

Along the way, make Your purpose clear
in all the plans You bring.
Along the way, may Your Spirit be the source of everything.
Give me guidance and direction in the choices that I make.
When my path becomes uncertain, help redeem any mistakes.
Along the way, shine Your light in me so others will see You.

Give me hope and inspiration to be all that I can be
and a vision that is greater than the obstacles I see.
Along the way, shine Your light in me so others will see You.
Along the way, shine Your light in me so others will see You.

---

[3] When I wrote this song, I wanted to convey that when people look at me, it's more important for them to see the Light of Jesus shining in me than to see me.

CHAPTER NINE

CONFIRMATIONS

On the Monday morning after this incredibly eventful week-end, I had to face the busy workweek ahead. In addition to committing any spare time I had to prayer, I planned to devote my energy to unravelling the mystery of how God reveals Himself. To me, the best place to discover the answer was in the Bible.

The first thing I needed God to confirm was my experience of inviting Jesus into my heart. Surely, I thought, there would be a similar situation recorded somewhere between Genesis and Revelation. I wasn't very familiar with scripture, but I knew how important the Gospels were. They seemed to be the obvious place to start.

I opened my Bible at Matthew, but nothing I read even vaguely mirrored what had happened to me. I then finished reading the remaining Gospels, which took several days.

Still, I felt no confirmation from God.

I forged ahead, reading everything from Acts to Galatians, which took many weeks. My prayers went unanswered. And so did my questions.

God only knows what kept me going and why I didn't feel discouraged.

I'm forever thankful that I read the next letter of the Apostle Paul. As I read the first chapter of Ephesians, the words spoke to me in a personal, refreshing way:

And you too, when you had heard the message of the truth, the good news of your salvation, and had believed it, became incorporate in Christ and received the seal of the promised Holy Spirit; and that Spirit is the pledge that we shall enter upon our heritage, when God has redeemed what is his own, to his praise and glory.

Because of all this, now that I have heard of the faith you have in the Lord Jesus and of the love you bear towards all God's people, I never cease to give thanks for you when I mention you in my prayers. (Ephesians 1:13–16)

The phrase "all God's people," I remembered, were the words Mark had written on the piece of paper after I'd spoken in tongues. Except Mark had written it as "all *My* people," because the message had come from God.

And then the confirmation came! When I read the next few verses, the words practically jumped off the page:

I pray that the God of our Lord Jesus Christ, the all-glorious Father, may give you the spiritual powers of wisdom and vision, by which there comes the knowledge of him. I pray that your inward eyes may be illumined, so that you may know what is the hope to which he calls you, what the wealth and glory of the share he offers you among his people in their heritage, and how vast the resources of his power open to us who trust in him. (Ephesians 1:17–19)

Where Paul writes, *"I pray that your inward eyes may be illumined,"* he is describing almost exactly what I experienced. It's also the same thing I described to John about the dazzling light I'd seen while my eyes were closed. No monarch's crown jewels could ever match the magnificence of that light; it was beyond description.

Of course, I hadn't really known this was a vision from God until reading Ephesians.

Another confirmation came later in the passage, where trust is mentioned. As I waited in the prayer line, I had told God that I was trusting Him one hundred percent to come into my life.

Here is how I understand Ephesians 1:19–20. As Christians, God is more than willing and able to give us the vast resources of His infinite power to equip us to spread the good news of our salvation to the ends of the earth.

When I meditate on these verses, I think of Paul describing what I refer to as resurrection power. He writes that the resources of God's power are open to those who trust in Him:

> They are measured by his strength and the might which he exerted in Christ when he raised him from the dead, when he enthroned him at his right hand in the heavenly realms… (Ephesians 1:19–20)

Let me repeat: that's clearly resurrection power!

We are the hands and feet of Christ. And just as surely as the sun will rise tomorrow, we can do immeasurably more to further His cause. But we can't do it alone. The sooner we acknowledge that reality, the sooner we can let Jesus lead as we obediently follow.

Before I continue sharing my story, I am reminded that you also have a story to tell. Whether you're at the beginning, in the middle, or writing the final chapter, it is never too late to let God direct your path and guide you to where you are meant to be. He leads and you follow. His plan for your life won't come to fruition any other way. When you humble yourself, God alone gets the glory.

Maybe you've tried many times to overcome a difficult situation or persistent obstacle, but you've felt powerless. When that happens, it's usually because you're trying to carry the burden and fix a problem by yourself. But you were never meant to do this. Only the Carpenter who hung on the cross, whose hands were pierced with nails, is strong enough to carry the sins of the world. Only He can carry our burdens as we cast our cares upon Him.

If you're facing an uncertain future, you are not alone. God is right there, waiting for you to lean on Him. Like me, maybe you have a wounded heart, but He can transform your life and give you a healed Spirit. Begin your journey today. Victory awaits!

CHAPTER TEN

SHARING THE GOOD NEWS

No book of the Bible has spoken to me more than Paul's letter to the Ephesians. From the very first time I set my eyes on its impactful message, it continues to reveal *"the good news of the unfathomable riches of Christ…"* (Ephesians 3:8).

This is the message I wanted so desperately to share with my mom and two sisters in North Bay. Even before becoming a Christian, I had routinely phoned my mom at least weekly from Kitchener. But since committing my life to Christ, my phone calls to her had substantially increased in frequency and duration. I trusted that God would help me plant the seed of faith in their hearts, especially my mom's. Of all people, she deserved to feel the warmth of God's love and discover that she could invite Jesus into her life.

But that presented a formidable challenge for me. I wondered when the next Christian conference would be held in Kitchener. Was there an upcoming event I could invite my mom to in Kitchener, to meet Pastor Gord? As I tried to make this plan a reality, I recognized that the logistics involved would prove insurmountable. I needed to find another solution, and days passed as I pondered how to connect my mom with Pastor Gord.

Until this point, I naively believed he was the only person in the western hemisphere who could tell my mom about Jesus and lead her in prayer to receive Him. Then I read Romans 10:11–17:

Scripture says, "Everyone who has faith in him will be saved from shame"—everyone: there is no distinction between Jew and Greek, because the same Lord is Lord of all, and is rich enough for the need of all who invoke him. For everyone, as it says again—"everyone who invokes the name of the Lord will be saved". How could they invoke one in whom they had no faith? And how could they have faith in one they had never heard of? And how hear without someone to spread the news? And how could anyone spread the news without a commission to do so? And that is what Scripture affirms: "How welcome are the feet of the messengers of good news!"

But not all have responded to the good news. For Isaiah says, "Lord, who has believed our message?" We conclude that faith is awakened by the message, and the message that awakens it comes through the word of Christ.

I studied this passage diligently and kept gleaning the same message: I was the one God had chosen to lead my mom in prayer to receive Jesus! It was crystal-clear. There was no doubt in my mind; my mom would be far more receptive to me than a perfect stranger.

Then I recalled the interpretation Mark had received when I spoke in the unfamiliar language at the conference. Part of the message the Holy Spirit gave him was about me and John ministering to my family.

Ordinarily I would have shrunk from such a challenge, but everything had changed in the past month. I felt like a brand-new creation. I had received a spiritual makeover. My previous lack of confidence had been replaced with boldness. My courage had been reborn from knowing who I was in Christ. I was no longer the quiet introvert who didn't have a purpose. I had given Jesus all my feelings of unworthiness and inadequacy.

Instead of hearing my dad's voice echo in my mind, telling me I wasn't good enough, I was listening to a new voice. The words of the Good Shepherd had never sounded more welcoming. And never had I possessed such bold confidence before. My fears had been erased. I believed that God could use even me to help spread His message.

With my newfound conviction, I phoned my mom and made a reservation to travel by train to North Bay. Planning to arrive for the upcoming weekend, I packed my suitcase and lay my Bible right on top before closing it.

I was fortunate enough to have Friday off work so I could spend most of the day travelling. After leaving Kitchener, I made a brief stop to change trains in Toronto. By early evening, I was thrilled to look out the window to see the train pulling into the North Bay station.

Before long I was knocking on my sister's front door, where I would stay for the weekend. It was getting late and both of us were tired, so it made sense to hold off any conversation about God until after we'd had a good night's rest.

The next morning began with a hearty breakfast. Then we waited for my younger sister to arrive. With our family history, there was lots to talk about, meaning that my morning Evangelism 101 presentation stretched into the afternoon. Both sisters seemed receptive to the message of faith.

When it was time to pray, one at a time I gently laid my hands on their heads and led them to receive Jesus. As they each repeated the prayer, the Holy Spirit fell upon them and they couldn't remain standing.

Inviting Jesus into their lives was the first step in a brand-new journey of faith for both. I prayed that this deeply personal experience would be the foundation for them to nurture their relationship with God.

After lots of tears and hugs, my thoughts promptly turned to my mom. I needed to get together with her soon, because the next day was Sunday and I would be taking the early train back home.

I kept phoning her, but she didn't answer. Hours passed, and when I eventually reached her I learned that she and my dad had been in a car accident on the outskirts of town. She assured me that they were okay, but I could hear in her voice that she was badly shaken.

We decided to see each other the next day.

In order to have time to tell her about Jesus, I would now need to put Plan B into action. I cancelled my train ticket and booked a new reservation, which would take me home on the midnight train instead. I could sleep on the train as long as I made sure to be awake to catch the connecting train in Toronto and then get to work promptly Monday morning.

No problem, I thought. *Done.*

On Sunday morning, my mom and I agreed to get together at my parents' home after lunch. It seemed like the perfect time—or, better said, the only time—since my dad wouldn't be home. Mentioning God to him would just ignite his anger, upsetting us and destroying any chance of peace. I knew there was a very brief window of opportunity for me to pray with my mom to receive Jesus. And with every passing hour, that window was slowly closing.

Minutes after I watched my dad get into his car and drive away, my mom opened the front door and welcomed me with open arms. We sat at the kitchen table and I finally had a chance to talk about Jesus. She and her brother and sister had grown up in a Christian family. Faith had been an important part of their lives. They had also been musical and often sang at church until they became young adults and moved away from home.

They'd also endured their share of tragedy. A younger brother had died at the age of ten from a childhood illness. And one Christmas Eve, my mom's dad was killed by a drunk driver while walking home from church. The accident had happened on a concession road near Leamington. Although I never got the chance to meet either of my grandparents on my mother's side, from all the wonderful stories it seemed she had been blessed and deeply loved.

I knew that my mom believed in God. She had a simple yet unwavering faith and prayed often. If not for her faith and prayers, I'm not sure she ever would have survived the persistent years of undeserved verbal and physical abuse at the hands of my dad.

As a child, I never heard my dad speak a kind word to my mom. I never saw him hug her, or even smile at her. He never gave her flowers on her birthday; he never gave her anything except heartache, nightmares, broken eyeglasses, black and blue bruises that faded, and emotional scars that didn't. No wonder her self-worth was as frail as a tattered ragdoll.

But deep inside my mom's tender-hearted soul, I prayed there was a glimmer of hope. She needed her poverty of spirit to be eclipsed by the pure joy of knowing God. I wanted my mom, this broken vessel, to be made whole again. When she invited Jesus to come into her life, I prayed she would be set free to feel the warmth and light of Jesus shining within her.

This made me think of a scripture I had read soon after receiving Jesus:

> For the same God who said, "Out of darkness let
> light shine", has caused his light to shine within

us, to give the light of revelation—the revelation
of the glory of God in the face of Jesus Christ. (2
Corinthians 4:6)

Soon we would be praying. But this wasn't my moment, or
even my mom's. It was God's moment. And I was pretty sure it was
going to be memorable.

As I sat face to face with my mom, I thought about all the
prayers God must be answering. He was faithfully responding to
a multitude of requests from every corner of the planet. I just had
to trust that He would also somehow answer the call to be our
invited guest at this modest kitchen table in North Bay, Ontario.

If I had learned anything, it was that God could do the
impossible. We were in good hands.

We bowed our heads and then I took both of my mom's hands
in mine and asked her to repeat the same prayer I was going to say.
I can still hear her voice in my head as she prayed softly, humbly,
and sincerely.

When we finished, silence filled the air. Then my mom shared
that when she had started to pray, a penetrating heat had enveloped
her. It had felt like flames of fire, and it hadn't been scary. I then
explained to her that a flame was one of many symbols in the Bible
referring to the Holy Spirit. She had felt God was speaking to her,
welcoming her into His family.

Our precious time together that afternoon ended. But before
I left, I gave my mom a Bible I had bought for her, identical to
mine. I had written various scriptures on pieces of paper and
placed them inside at the appropriate places. They were easy to
understand. I wanted her to become familiar with God's Word
and take comfort in these special verses.

The occasion was cause for great celebration! My mom's future
looked better than her past.

We still had many years together, but after she passed away John and I cleaned her house—and on the bedroom night table, we noticed her Bible. All those scripture references were still inside, with one addition: a little note in her own handwriting that said,

> On May 31, 1979, I received Jesus Christ and the Holy Spirit into my heart. Glory be to God for He has and will take all my burdens upon Himself. I am and will be a better living Christian for I have Jesus truly in my heart. I know now that I can overcome any obstacle in my life. Thank you. Amen.

I didn't realize until reading my mom's precious note that she had received Jesus just one month after I had. That reality was astonishing to me. It confirmed that Jesus had impacted my life so profoundly in such a short time that I'd felt an eager willingness to share about Him so my mom could experience that joy too.

CHAPTER ELEVEN

THE PRAIRIES

The next milestone we celebrated was John's ordination in the spring of 1981. He had completed his combined master's degree. In addition to being a joyous occasion, it also meant we would soon be moving. Somewhere.

It was a bittersweet time. We had made some incredibly close friendships through our involvement at the seminary and within our congregation. Our bond with the church youth group had deepened over the years as we nurtured them through many activities: preparing and conducting worship services, taking them to hear Christian speakers and singers, attending youth retreats in southern Ontario, going out for social gatherings with other youth groups, and most of all guiding them to seek a closer relationship with God through Jesus Christ.

As we attended many farewell events, saying goodbye proved more difficult than we could have imagined. It was especially emotional for me to leave the place where I had experienced the dramatic birth pangs of my faith. John also felt a certain sadness to part ways with the congregation that was so proud of him as an ordinand and where he had preached his first sermon. And yet we both realized that these experiences had helped prepare us for whatever lay ahead, regardless of where we went next.

While waiting to hear where the church would settle us, we prayed about three different possibilities: Newfoundland, the Northwest Territories, and Saskatchewan.

Our choice was Saskatchewan, a vast expanse where grain elevators dot the landscape, where fields of gold rise to kiss the sky. We had heard about how approaching thunderstorms and accompanying waves of lightning can seem to dance across the invading twilight. A bonus was that Mark and Patty had recently accepted a call to central Saskatchewan. Hopefully we would be neighbours again.

Our prayers were answered! While ministering in the prairie towns of Neville, Cadillac, and Vanguard for nearly three years, God blessed us in immeasurable ways, none greater than the birth of our son, Joshua Ryan.

In 1984, before Josh blew out the candles on his second birthday cake, John had accepted a new call, this time to Moose Jaw. Prior to moving, though, my parents decided to drive from North Bay and visit us in Neville. It was good to see them and reconnect. It was even better to introduce them to their new grandson!

They spent several days with us. Even though much joyfulness prevailed, because of Josh, I was able to hide my deep sadness at the thought of the huge emotional chasm that existed between my dad and me. As far back as I could remember, our conversations had been superficial. I'm not sure why I had hoped things might be different now.

While they were our guests, my parents settled right into our slower pace of life. We explained to them how, at harvest, the relaxed rhythm transitioned into weeks of hurried activity with unbroken hours of daily toil. At times we would see the combines work through the night, their lights glowing in the dark and resembling fireflies on the horizon.

As we took my parents for a casual walk around town, we pointed out the most important and busiest establishment, the place where all the neighbours gathered: the coffee shop. There were no introductions needed, though, since the people we encountered there already knew who my parents were and where they were from. Besides, Neville only had a population of one hundred, but their hospitality personified the true spirit of the West.

The day soon arrived when my parents decided to begin their trip back to North Bay. We stood in the driveway and waved goodbye as we watched them pursue the ribbon of road that soon stretched out of sight. I now had a heart full of new memories to reminisce about.

As I reflected on our time together, it brought me great peace to know that my mom had developed a genuine relationship with Christ. This had been evident in our recent conversations, as well as the inner strength I noticed in her.

But I could see beyond my dad's façade. I knew that an aching emptiness must be devouring him inside.

With our move to Moose Jaw circled on the calendar—it was only a couple of weeks away—we still had lots of boxes to pack. Both John and I worked diligently, taking turns entertaining an active one-and-a-half-year-old. Or more accurately, Josh was providing the entertainment for us.

Instead of focusing on any number of things, like John's next ministry opportunity, moving to a new city, or the chance to make wonderful new friends, a persistent thought held my mind hostage: I couldn't talk to my dad about God, but maybe I could write a letter and share how He had changed my life. In my letter, I could take the time to explain how much God loved him. Indeed, how much He had always loved him, even though nobody had ever told him.

There had to be a way for me to share about Jesus too, for my dad to invite Him into his heart. Before I could even begin this monumental pursuit, though, I needed to wrap myself in prayer and ask God to give me His guidance. There had to be some words I could summon to penetrate my dad's hard outer shell.

After praying, I sat down at the kitchen table and wrote the most difficult letter of my life—difficult only in the sense that whatever I wrote would have to be a delicate way of conveying the good news of God's love and highlighting some easy-to-understand scriptures that supported the message. None of my journalism assignments at college had come close to tasking me with such a herculean challenge.

I wrote the letter and mailed it. We moved. And I wish I didn't have to say it ended there. But it ended there.

My mom told me that my dad wouldn't even read the letter. But she read it and confirmed that it had been clear to her that every word was guided by God's hand and the Holy Spirit. She had been able to feel love spilling from every page. My mom said that she wept, feeling hurt and disappointed that my dad wouldn't even give the letter a chance.

He wouldn't even give God a chance.

God has so much love to give, but it's like a box of chocolates, as the popular expression goes: we can either admire it from afar and imagine how sweet it is, or we can *"Taste, then, and see that the Lord is good"* (Psalm 34:8). The choice is ours.

But I've never met a person who's worse off for indulging in chocolate.

CHAPTER TWELVE

SIXTEEN DAYS

More than three years passed and we settled nicely into our busy life in Moose Jaw.

Out of the blue, my parents decided to take another trip out west. There were lots of tourist things to do in our new city and I loved making tasty recipes for the family. To make things even more fun, Josh had become a chattering four-year-old who could now call my mom and dad the endearing names of *Grandma* and *Grandpa*.

While my parents visited, John spent a lot of time listening to my dad talk about sports, particularly anything involving his favourite football teams or, of course, the Toronto Blue Jays. Meanwhile, my mom and I were content to take Josh for short walks down the street and around the neighbourhood. I still cherish the memory of Josh's little hand grasping my mom's hand, strolling together at a pace that suited them both.

After spending several days with us, the time came to say farewell and wish them safe travels back to North Bay. We all agreed that the next time we got together it would be our turn to make the long trek to Ontario.

My mom and I couldn't have been closer. We shared a deep bond of faith and could talk about it freely. We often spoke about prayer too and how wonderful it felt to have a direct line to God. We needed that constant connection in our lives.

As for my dad, I couldn't say we had a close relationship, but at least there was an absence of bitterness and anger. Since my teenage years, I had tried to understand how one person could be filled with such emptiness. Looking back, it seemed to me that my dad felt entitled to unleash his wrath on those around him. The only conclusion I could come to was that his parents hadn't known how to love him. I suspect they had, at times, treated him worse than an animal. Because that's how he treated us.

Part of me felt sorry for my dad. Another part of me thought he should have known better. Regardless of the state of our relationship, I decided to let the Serenity Prayer be my guide. I must admit that since John and I had moved to Kitchener, gotten married, travelled to our new home in Saskatchewan, and had Josh, our interactions with my dad had at least been civil, bordering on enjoyable.

Days after my parents arrived back in North Bay, my mom phoned to say that they'd had a safe trip. It was good to hear her voice! She thanked us for making them both feel so welcome and we made sure to keep in touch often, either by phoning each other or by what has become the lost art of writing letters.

My mom also reminded me that it was our turn to travel east next time. I assured her that we were indeed planning to make the trip, probably sometime in the next year.

It was already June and we had barely a month before Josh would be enjoying his long-awaited holidays from school. The carefree days of summer would spoil us and John was looking forward to a more relaxed worship routine at church.

As for myself, I had become an avid flower gardener, rising with the sun many mornings to weed and water the delicate blossoms before the heat and humidity made their appearance.

That's where I was when I heard the phone ring.

I managed to brush off some of the soil on my gardening shoes and made my way to the phone in the kitchen. When I answered, my mom told me that my dad had had a stroke. He was in the hospital and all she really knew was that the stroke seemed to be major.

All I could do was try my best to calm her down and offer words of comfort. Besides me, the only other person around to help my mom through this would be her next-door neighbour and best friend, Jean. Various events over the last few years had caused irreconcilable differences to arise between my sisters and my mom, and consequently between my sisters and me. Suffice it to say that they had both disowned her and no longer wanted to be part of her life. Or mine.

How many of us become disillusioned after we become Christians, disappointed that our problems don't just evaporate and disappear? But we don't live in a utopia. As we mature in our walk of faith and study of God's Word, we realize that Jesus never said our lives would be free of problems. We are promised no shortage of heartache, pain, or suffering. However, we can be forever thankful that He meets us where we're at and empowers us with His Spirit to rise above the challenges and claim victory in His name. He prepares us for the storms of life when we don't even know they're coming.

My mom had already weathered a barrage of hardship, and I knew I needed to be there as she faced the uncertainty of my dad's declining health. I wanted to be there for my dad too. The only assurance I needed was that God would be there when I walked into his hospital room.

After talking things over with John, I phoned my mom to let her know I would catch the earliest flight I could. John and Josh planned to drive to North Bay after school ended in June.

Flying wasn't my favourite mode of transportation. Anyone who knew me well would have known that had they ever seen me in an airport, it wasn't because I was a prospective passenger. I like to keep my feet on the ground. But there I was, standing in line with all the other travellers.

It was hard saying goodbye to John and Josh at the airport in Regina. I was especially sad that I wouldn't be there to see Josh on his last day of school. That had always been a favourite time of celebration for our family, saying goodbye to the memories of one year and anticipating what the next would bring.

As I boarded my flight, I had a lot to think about. I could hardly wait to see my mom and start relieving some of the stress she must be feeling.

The flight to Toronto, and subsequently to North Bay, was uneventful and the runway at the North Bay airport was a welcome sight; soon my feet would touch the ground again.

My parents lived in Ferris, a newer suburb on the south side of the city. It was about ten miles from the airport and I would have to take a bus there, since I didn't have use of a car. I looked forward to seeing all the quaint shops that I knew lined the streets and the familiar places I had frequented years before.

I got off the bus on Lakeshore Drive and enjoyed a brief walk to my parents' house, where my mom was standing at the front window, waiting. She greeted me at the side door. The aroma of freshly brewed coffee and homemade baking was calling my name.

Sitting at the kitchen table, I listened to her recall the events before my dad had suffered the stroke. So far the doctors hadn't given my mom any indication that he was making progress or would get better. He had already lost nearly eighty pounds and the hospital staff were just trying to make him feel comfortable.

We decided to catch an early afternoon bus to the hospital. I was thankful that I wouldn't be alone when I saw my dad the first time. After that, I planned to visit him by myself so my mom could get the rest she needed.

The bus dropped us off near the hospital. As we took the short walk to the front door, I felt my anxiety building. I braced myself for whatever was about to happen. I knew my mom needed me to be strong. So did my dad.

When we walked into his room, my dad was lying in bed, looking straight ahead with a blank stare on his face. I gently approached, took his hand, and hugged him. That's when I heard him say my name. My mom had prepared me for this, explaining that he had regained his speech but spoke very slowly.

I remembered to speak slowly in return, to make it easier for him to understand.

I told him about my flight and, of course, that John and Josh were still in Moose Jaw so Josh could finish his school year. I didn't want to overstay my welcome or exhaust my dad, so we left after a brief visit but made sure he knew I'd be back in the morning.

After we said goodbye and left the room, we had only taken a few steps into the hall when a nurse approached us. This seemed like the perfect opportunity to talk with her about my dad's prognosis.

"He's dying," she said emphatically after a brief chat.

I wasn't prepared for the emotional earthquake that shook every fibre of my body. As a Christian, I was used to holding on to hope, even when a situation seemed hopeless.

On the bus ride back to my parents' house, my mom sat in silence, speechless. I reached to the depths of my being, determined not to let the nurse's words deflate me.

Morning couldn't come early enough. This wounded warrior had another battle to fight. If only I could convince my dad he had a chance of getting better. If only I could get that lion inside him to rise and fight for his life—and I knew there was a lion inside; I had heard it roar many times! If only I could persuade the doctors and nurses not to give up on him, that maybe his situation could turn around.

If only.

The bus ride to the hospital took about a half-hour. I planned to make this part of my routine every morning. Afterward I would return to spend time with my mom before repeating the trip to see my dad before I fed him dinner.

When I walked into his hospital room this time, he was sitting up in an easy chair near the window. I sat and talked with him for a while. I noticed that his hair wasn't combed and wondered how recently it had been washed. I asked if he would like me to wash it and he seemed happy for me to do that. All I needed was a basin of warm water, shampoo, and a dry towel. I just had to lay his head back in the chair and pour the shampoo and water over it, a simple task to make him feel better. After a quick comb of his hair, he looked fabulous.

It seemed only natural now for me to give him a shave, since I could see no one had remembered to do it. This only took a few minutes. I followed it with a complete face and hand washing. That was time well spent!

Lunch arrived before too long and I realized there was no way for him to feed himself. I would have assumed someone, probably a nurse, would have fed him breakfast as time allowed. I reminded myself to inquire about this.

Even though I was focusing on each task at hand, the thought kept replaying in my mind: *See, Dad? This is what you do when you love someone.*

I found myself wondering how it was humanly possible for me to take care of my dad after the life I had known living under his roof. And then I knew: there weren't just two of us in that hospital room; God was amidst us. Only the power of His love filling me, helping me to forgive the past, enabled me to so lovingly care for my dad. I wasn't just going through the motions; this was God's uncon-ditional love in action, love that had been poured out on the cross.

At that point, I noticed that my dad seemed exhausted. He struggled to sit up in the chair, so I asked the nurses if they could move him back into bed. I felt he would fall asleep in no time, which he promptly did.

Having lots of time to catch the next bus, I decided to take a few minutes and sit down near the window while my dad slept. Now it was my turn to stare into space and relive the hours that had just transpired. In a million years, I wouldn't have believed this was how the final chapter of my dad's life would be written, with me taking care of him in his hour of need.

As I continued to gaze out the window, I had no idea what may lie ahead. I didn't know what I might need to do for him—or more importantly, what I might need to do for my heavenly Father. I closed my eyes and laid all the decades of hurt at the foot of the cross, and left them there. Then and only then, as God helped me let go of painful memories, was I able to hold on to the hope that there were better memories to be made.

I take no credit for that triumph. I'm no martyr. God is the One who moved, who acted. I simply surrendered to Him. I asked God to flood my heart with His love so I could share the overflowing love with my dad.

When we empty ourselves to let God fill us, we are to truly *empty* ourselves. Not partway. One hundred percent empty. By attempting to accomplish great things for God and minister to others, we can achieve either partial or whole results. When Jesus died on the cross, He didn't suffer unbearable anguish for half the world; He endured that torment for the whole world.

Nothing we do for God can ever be done halfway and be called a victory. He demands more of us, even from an unlikely follower of Jesus. How can we demand any less?

Nearly two weeks passed and I continued taking the bus twice a day to the hospital. My visits with my dad became a routine. I needed to make sure he was washed and that he had lunch and dinner, although his appetite had greatly diminished.

One day he asked me when John and Josh would be coming to see him.

"Today," I replied.

That brought a smile to his face.

As if right on queue, they walked in just a short time later. I could tell he was excited to see them and the long-awaited reunion brought him great joy. They spent as much time with him as they could before my dad got tired.

Afterward we left to see my mom at home. That was another reunion of great celebration. Amidst the bleak days that surrounded us, joyfulness and even some laughter echoed off the walls of my parents' home. How good it was to see John and Josh being able to bring a twinkle to my mom's eyes!

The next morning, John dropped me off at the hospital and planned to pick me up later. I wanted he and Josh to spend some quality time with my mom, who had often been by herself. I hoped this would bring a sense of normalcy to her life, even if it was just a temporary distraction from my dad's uncertain future. Tomorrow would come soon enough.

When I arrived to greet my dad the next morning, I barely had enough time to speak because he clearly had something important to say. He told me about a dream he'd had the night before. As he looked toward the window, he described the dream.

He had found himself alone, cold, and lost in a dark, damp wilderness, frightened to be cut off from everything and not knowing how to free himself.

My dad was visibly distressed while telling me this. He was convinced he had really been to this place.

CHAPTER TWELVE: SIXTEEN DAYS

The dream didn't make much sense to me—that is, until I saw my dad the next day. Again, as soon as I entered his room, he became very animated and told me about another dream he'd had.

This time, the setting was very peaceful and soothing. He had seen a long, elaborate banquet table covered with a crisp white linen. The table was colossal in length because of the multitudes of people expected at the coming feast.

When the banquet was ready to begin, a sense of anticipation and excitement building, everyone stood waiting for the special guest of honour to arrive.

After listening to both intriguing dreams, I clearly understood their purpose. I believe God had revealed Himself to my dad in both situations, giving him a glimpse of what hell was like as well as inviting him to the banquet table to meet Jesus.

But I still didn't understand the timing of my dad's dreams. However, that revelation came before the next sunrise.

In the evening, John and I brought Josh with us to see my dad. It was good for all of us to be together and let him know that we loved him. Few words were spoken, but our presence seemed to bring him much comfort. I'm sure he could sense us in the room and the love our hearts held for him.

My dad died that night on Tuesday, July 5, 1988. He was only sixty-nine years old, which seems like such a young age at which to leave this world.

I have often reflected on the time I had with my dad before he died. From the day my flight left Regina to my last good-bye to him, we had sixteen days. That period was a gift—if not for my dad, it was for me.

I believe God allowed me to have those sixteen days because He knew that was all the time I would need to bring healing to the otherwise fractured relationship. I had only needed to use that precious time wisely. I never considered using it to engage in superficial chatter about the weather or sports. Rather, taking care of my dad helped me to realize that we need to speak to those we love about the important things in life, the things that matter. Whether someone we love is dying or in optimum health, isn't it better to show them how much they mean to us here and now, instead of at their funeral? Isn't it better to bring someone flowers today and hand the bouquet to them in person, rather than laying flowers beside an engraved stone surrounded by overgrown grass?

We can't allow ourselves to be lulled into complacency, believing we'll have that important conversation with our beloved family or friends some other day. That may be our hope, and it is noble, but that's not reality. I'm reminded of the familiar phrase that tells us, "God laughs when we make plans."

Life is not a dress rehearsal. We may not have sixteen days to spend with someone we love; we may not even have one day. I didn't with my brother, David.

Looking back, I hope and pray that my dad saw the time I took care of him as a gift. Maybe someday I'll know, or maybe I'll never know. Through my words and actions, I know that I did everything possible to bring God's love into my dad's hospital room, as well as into his heart, mind, and soul. God gave him the dreams, which were obviously meant to invite a timely response. I don't know what path my dad chose. But I do know that the choice wasn't hard.

God gives us that same choice every day, but too many of us ignore His offer. And if we do decide to accept Jesus Christ, we mistakenly believe we must wait until our last breath before experiencing His love and presence.

That couldn't be further from the truth. Jesus knocks at the door of our heart twenty-four hours per day. How patient He is with us! Today is the only day we have, and only a fool would dismiss the knock at the door if they knew who it was and the promises He could deliver. It's the most important door we'll ever open.

Jesus is waiting to give us many gifts to nurture an abundant, purposeful life. But something doesn't become a gift until it changes hands. We cannot allow the knock at the door to go unanswered.

SIXTEEN DAYS

Sixteen days was all we had before your life was through.
Just one last chance for us to say "I care" and "I love you."

Sixteen days, I asked myself; why does my father have to die?
And through the sorrow and the pain,
it even hurt too much to cry.

Sixteen days of endless hope, when death
was all around your room.
The only thought that kept me sane:
I knew that God was with us too.

Sixteen days of memories, the way I watched you fight to live.
We didn't share a lifetime, but I'll cherish all that you could give.

Sixteen days of sunrises, I never felt the light of day.
I faced the truth that haunts me still,
that death would soon take you away.

Sixteen days, that's not enough for you
to share your life with me.
But I will wait with patience, Dad, for we will have eternity.

CHAPTER THIRTEEN

TRANSITIONS

People often say that God's timing is perfect. It would be callous to say that death is convenient, but because my dad passed away in early July we were afforded the opportunity to spend extra time with my mom, time we otherwise wouldn't have had. John was able to take much of his holidays and Josh wouldn't start school until September.

We stayed with my mom for nearly two weeks, making sure she felt settled and had enough confidence to move forward. She needed to create a new daily routine which included buying groceries, paying bills, maintaining the yard, and visiting her doctor if the need arose.

My mom didn't drive, so it was another blessing to have her closest friend, Jean, right next door. They had been getting together to have coffee for several years, but occasionally Jean had taken my mom out, even if only for a change of scenery. I knew that as long as Jean didn't change her address, my mom needn't worry about anything.

As we drove back to Moose Jaw, I couldn't help but wonder how my mom really felt without my dad at home. I hoped she wouldn't feel alone, but most of her marriage had been overshadowed by loneliness, her most loyal companion in life; she wouldn't need to become reacquainted with the feeling. And

I was sure she wouldn't miss the daily orders from my dad to have his breakfast, lunch, and dinner on the table when he demanded. Maybe she would even feel relieved of the everyday duties that had previously consumed most of her time.

When we arrived home, I made sure to be diligent in keeping in touch. We talked on the phone at least twice a week and both enjoyed writing letters. From what I could glean, she seemed to be doing well. She enjoyed her newfound freedom of sleeping in at times, being able to watch her favourite TV programs, and eating whatever she wanted without adhering to a strict schedule. On rare occasions, she could even order takeout. She loved sitting on the back deck, soaking up rays of soothing sunshine. When we chatted, her contagious laughter sometimes echoed through the telephone.

My mom had lived her life by the golden rule, often doing without things she needed in order to help others. If I had to describe her, I would say that her personality was a combination of Mother Teresa and Phyllis Diller. It was clear to me that a new dawn was beckoning her to reclaim her spirit, which had remained dormant too long. It did my heart good to watch this beautiful butterfly spread her wings, soar to new heights, and finally escape the cocoon that had held her hostage.

Life on the prairies was going through a transition of its own; summer was about to bid farewell, with the onslaught of dusty combines gathering the bounty of the awaited harvest. As if by an artist's paintbrush, the thick green foliage that had once cloaked the trees was transformed into hues of crimson and gold.

Exciting changes were also happening in my career. I was offered the position of lifestyles editor at the local daily newspaper and continued in that job for nearly five years. I took every opportunity possible to feature stories about the Christian faith, including personal experiences in my weekly column, "That's

Life." I was incredibly thankful to have such a broad platform from which to share and witness about God.

Speaking of gratitude, we would soon celebrate Thanksgiving. Although abundantly aware how blessed we were, this time of year was still a poignant reminder of the loss our family had suffered. Yet I never doubted God's presence in our lives and His unfailing love.

A few months passed, and before we knew it a light dusting of snow had carpeted the ground and Yuletide songs were ringing in our ears. For our family, Christmas was the highlight of the year as we celebrated the Messiah's birth and the rebirth of God's love in our hearts!

The carols of the season were soon replaced by the spirited renditions of Auld Lang Syne and a blank page on our January calendar. We didn't know what the future held, but we knew Who held it.

During the holidays, we enjoyed lots of extra phone calls with my mom. I had recently talked to her and wished her a happy new year, so I was slightly surprised when she contacted me a couple of days later. Regardless, it was always a treat to be on the receiving end of her phoning us.

As soon as I heard her speak, though, it was clear that something was wrong. It was time for me to be a good listener, because I could hear the urgency in her voice, and maybe even a little fear.

My mom proceeded to tell me that Jean had just brought her home from a doctor's appointment. I recalled her mentioning to me weeks earlier that the big toe on her left foot had been quite painful; she thought there was either a cut or blister, but it wasn't healing. The toe had started to feel numb and look dark, convincing her to phone her family doctor.

Upon examination, he had advised her that she had gangrene and her left toe would need to be amputated. Because the foot was cold and the skin discoloured, her doctor also booked some imaging scans and blood tests. Until then, he had prescribed antibiotics to reduce the pain caused by the infection.

As we spoke, I chose my words wisely, hoping to console her. But I could tell she was distraught, which made two of us. All I could do was try to instill a sense of calm and somehow make her feel better. Being an eternal optimist and looking for the silver lining, I suggested that as unfortunate as the situation was, at least having the surgery would save her foot and subsequently her leg. I wouldn't have blamed her for disagreeing with me that this was a blessing.

Before I hung up, I asked her to stay in constant contact and keep me updated. To say I felt helpless would be an understatement, but hopeless I wasn't. In all things, no matter the circumstance, there's only one thing to do when you feel powerless, and that is get on your knees. Sometimes we consider prayer as a last resort. It should really be at the top of our priority list. Since becoming a Christian, I had learned that prayer isn't just about repeating empty words that evaporate into thin air. Besides the gift of love, I believe that prayer is the next best gift we can give someone.

Praying and waiting became my daily practice in the days that followed. Waiting is difficult at the best of times, but it's especially virtuous when it involves scheduling medical tests and receiving results.

I was perplexed enough wondering about the details of my mom's health, so I could only imagine what she was going through. It seemed like an eternity passed after our last conversation, so I decided to phone her early one morning.

I'm glad I did. It was so good to hear her voice.

She told me that Jean had recently taken her for a CT scan, MRI, and all the blood tests. The doctor's office hadn't called yet with the results, which is why she hadn't phoned. That made perfect sense to me. I assured her that I'd be waiting day and night, and to phone me anytime.

So when she phoned back later that very afternoon, I was surprised.

As soon as I picked up the phone, I could hear her sobbing. Through all the sorrowful crying, it took a while before she could speak. In the meantime, I searched my mind for the most soothing words possible. I told her that no matter what happened, we would get through it together. I tried to reassure her that everything was going to be okay.

All I could do was wait until she was ready to speak.

After my call that morning, the doctor's office had phoned and asked her to come in early that afternoon. Jean had driven her there.

At the appointment, the doctor had explained that the gangrene was spreading up her left leg. To save her life, the leg would have to be amputated, probably just below the knee. Her surgery had already been booked for Monday evening, which was just a few days away.

Now we were both crying. I had to pinch myself to make sure this wasn't part of a horrific nightmare. I couldn't think of what to say. I was about as speechless as I'd ever been. There was no silver lining on the horizon.

After what turned out to be a long, candid conversation, before hanging up I told my mom that I'd call her the next day.

I don't think I slept at all that night. And in the morning, still reeling from the news, I procrastinated in phoning her. I wanted to be strong and ease her pain, but I didn't think I could do either.

As with my dad's health crisis, a parade of if-onlys infiltrated my mind, repeating themselves. It felt like a thick, relentless fog that wouldn't lift, clouding my thoughts. If only my mom had gone to the doctor when she'd first noticed the cut on her toe. If only she hadn't waited so many weeks to mention something to Jean. If only there had been an alternative to lower leg amputation.

The more these two little words, *if only*, threatened my sanity, the more they gave me a reality check. I couldn't dwell in the recent past. There was no turning back. The only option was to move forward.

So I picked up the phone.

Despite everything that had transpired in the last twenty-four hours, my mom was taking a tenacious approach to the whole situation. She confided that although she was afraid to have the surgery, she was more concerned about the steps to follow— literally. I understood completely why she would be preoccupied with her recovery and all the questions that involved. She especially wanted to know how long it would take before she could walk again, not to mention the whole process of being fitted with a prosthetic leg.

I had phoned my mom to encourage and calm her, but she was the one calming me. Since she was looking far beyond the surgery, I realized that meant she had hope for the future. She still had a purpose and a reason for living. She wasn't about to give up, even though she was seventy. This was hardly the first struggle she had faced. No doubt her decades of battle wounds had helped prepare her for this new adversity.

Jean would take her to the hospital on Sunday, then help her get settled and stay with her most of the day. And various preliminary tests needed to be done.

Knowing that Sunday would probably be very hectic, I resolved to wait until Monday morning to reach out again. Upon getting up that day, I noticed that I'd neglected the housework for too long. I had just completed some of the most obvious tasks when the phone rang.

When I heard my mom's gentle voice, it was all I could do to refrain from crying. Just weeks earlier she'd had nothing more to worry about than a small cut on her toe. We'd thought she might just need a course of antibiotics. Now she was facing the most momentous challenge imaginable: the partial loss of a leg.

We had the deepest conversation a mother and daughter could have and didn't leave anything unsaid. Even though my words seemed inadequate, I hoped and prayed that my mom knew how much I loved her.

I needed her to lean on me and draw from my strength to make it through the upcoming surgery. More importantly, I knew she was leaning on God to sustain her with the immeasurable courage only He could impart.

Before our conversation ended, I prayed aloud and committed myself to unceasing prayer, day and night. I would also be with her in spirit.

Then I told my mom that I loved her.

"Carol, I know you'll be as close as your prayers," she replied. "I have already felt them."

After our family dinner that night, John had to attend a church board meeting and Josh was getting together with a friend who lived across the street. Finally, it was quiet—the perfect opportunity to offer uninterrupted prayers for my mom.

We lived in a bilevel house and I was drawn to go into the stairwell to pray. Tears rolled down my cheeks as I pleaded with God to save my mom's life. Not even an earthquake could have shaken me from those stairs.

Undoubtedly, God knew all the hardships she had been through. Surely she, of all people, deserved a little more happiness, a little more time at home with us before He welcomed her into His house. God must have some purpose for her to have come so far. Maybe there were others whose lives she could touch after living through this ordeal.

My prayers that night were filled with desperate, gut-wrenching pleas that my heart's desire would somehow move God's heart to healing, life, and victory. And when I had surrendered every last ounce of breath I had in me, when I had nothing left to give and no more words to say, I sat there limp from exhaustion. I was emotionally bankrupt.

Wiping my drenched face, I noticed that two and a half hours had passed.

I literally fell into bed that night and didn't wake up until I smelled the fresh brewed coffee on Tuesday morning. By now my mom would have been moved from the recovery room back to her own hospital bed. Hopefully she'd be sleeping and getting all the rest she needed.

I wanted to talk to her more than anything, but I decided to wait until just before noon to phone her. Waiting wasn't easy. I noticed myself growing more impatient; the hands on the kitchen clock barely seemed to move. I kept glancing at the hospital phone number and my mom's room number, both of which I had now memorized.

When I couldn't wait any longer, I prayerfully decided to make the call. The phone rang longer than I wanted it to before I heard the sweetest voice on earth: my mom's. I could tell she was very weak and would no doubt be hoping to keep our conversation brief.

I had just begun telling her about my prayers when she interrupted me. She thanked me for visiting her in the hospital, for being there. Not knowing how to respond, I explained that I was still in Moose Jaw and couldn't have been there. Again, she just insisted that I had been there.

How could this be possible?

She explained that she'd been lying in bed waiting for the nurses to arrive to take her to surgery. She had only closed her eyes to rest because she hadn't slept much the night before. A few minutes later, she opened her eyes to the sight of me standing at her bedside. When our eyes met, a deep sense of peace and love surrounded her. That's when she knew she had nothing to fear; no matter what happened, everything was going to be okay. She had felt an overwhelming calmness and strength.

Soon after that, the nurses had arrived to bring her to surgery.

If God had taught me anything along my journey of faith, it was that He was a God of surprises! No matter what I may have surmised, I couldn't outthink, outimagine, outplan, outbless, or outdo Him. That's why He has three letters in His name and I don't.

Why should I have been so astonished that during my prayers of intercession God had chosen to give my mom a vision through the power of the Holy Spirit? Among other things, He is our Advocate and Comforter. That's God's nature. He does the impossible. The Bible is filled with God's supernatural manifestations, and Hebrews 13:8 tells us that *"Jesus Christ is the same yesterday, today, and for ever."* This means that God's power and presence transcend all time and space. His divine intervention doesn't end with the last chapter of Revelation.

At a Christian conference I had attended years earlier, a speaker had taught about the Word of God and how, as believers, we need to remind ourselves that God's supernatural nature is inherent. During his presentation, he asked the audience some specific questions, including this one: "Do you think miracles happen to those who don't believe in them?" He ended with these words, "God said it. I believe it. That settles it." And then he walked offstage to thunderous applause.

God's Word never changes. This means that the following is true, through the power of the Word:

...the blind recover their sight, the lame walk, the lepers are made clean, the deaf hear, the dead are raised to life, the poor are hearing the good news... (Matthew 11:5)

I will pour out upon everyone a portion of my spirit; and your sons and daughters shall prophesy; your young men shall see visions, and your old men shall dream dreams. (Acts 2:17)

It's beyond our understanding why some prayers are miraculously answered yet others may not seem to be. We don't know the reason. Here's why:

Now we see only puzzling reflections in a mirror, but then we shall see face to face. My knowledge now is partial; then it will be whole, like God's knowledge of me. (1 Corinthians 13:12)

God continues to reveal Himself in unexpected ways and unlikely places; His ways are not our ways.

I am so thankful that it wasn't too far from Moose Jaw to North Bay for a heavenly vision to be carried on angel's wings! God made certain that the image of me reached its destiny at the precise moment it was intended, and for the exact person it was meant for. His divine intervention knows no bounds!

Speaking of angels, as soon as my mom felt strong enough she was transferred on a flight to Toronto. For more than six weeks, she was a patient at a hospital specializing in treating amputees. Her rehabilitation included everything from fitting her with the proper prosthetic, learning how to walk, and participating in group sessions that dealt with loss.

I still have every letter she wrote to me from her hospital bed in Toronto. In some, it's clear that she felt the nurses and physical therapists were demanding too much of someone her age. It must have been difficult for my mom to be confronted with those expectations and write about them, because it was emotional for me to read.

Yet God had a higher purpose for her inside those dreary hospital walls. No doubt the light of my mom's faith shone bright.

When the therapists recognized how far she had come in her own rehabilitation, as well as her inner healing, they presented her with an inspiring opportunity. Among the amputees were several young men who for one reason or another had given up on life. Seeing no hope for the future, they had each purposely thrown themselves in front of an oncoming train. Because these young men had seen only hopelessness before their injuries, I could only imagine the unbearable pain they faced afterward as amputees.

Enter: my mom. Her story was inspiring, and she told them that if she could survive this setback, so could they. She was in the right place at the right time to encourage them. No professional motivational speaker could have had more of an impact on these young amputees, because she was one of them. She had walked a mile in their prosthetics and could meet them where they were at.

I'm sure God used her to reach other amputees in a mighty way. Like them, at times we may see ourselves as a victim of circumstance. But when we take the focus off our problems, God can use our witness to help minister to others.

Throughout my mom's time in Toronto, I wrote many letters and often spoke with her on the phone. In one conversation, she said that her progress was so remarkable that in a couple of days she would be taking a flight back to North Bay.

For the next six months, my mom got reacquainted with her home and learned how to navigate it inside and outside. Managing the stairs was especially challenging, but she was determined to be independent for as long as she could.

I tried to glean how she was really feeling and whether she was as healthy and optimistic as she sounded. That concern was soon answered when my mom said she wanted to take a trip to see us. Summer was the best time to see how well she had adapted.

Because so much distance separated us, we made sure to treat every day together as a special gift. Between all our laughter and my mom's hilarious antics, we also made time to share our faith and reflect on the many blessings God had bestowed on us. It was fun and gratifying to treat her like the queen she was, and at every chance we pampered her endlessly. It was a memorable summer for our family.

Years passed with our twice-weekly phone calls nurturing our bond. Because of her hurtful life, she had every reason to let bitterness and resentment cloud her vision and destroy her joy, yet she counted her blessings every day and welcomed God's love to light her path.

One particular night on the phone, my mom lamented the fact that she lived so far away. I told her that when she went to bed at night she saw the same moon in the sky as I did. We made a promise to say goodnight to each other while looking at the moon. I like to imagine there were moments when we were looking at the moon at the same time.

Many nights, I still feel that special connection to my mom. Even now, I love to go outside and gaze at the stars dancing across the midnight sky against their dark backdrop. I marvel at God's brilliant handiwork.

In my mom's latter years, she came to know God in a personal way. Although she had to wait a long time to experience that divine love, it was a blessing for her to realize that nothing and no one could ever separate her from it.

That same love embraced her when she passed from this world into the next on June 18, 1994.

After the funeral, before leaving her house for the last time, I was able to take the Bible with me that I had once bought for her. As I picked it up from the night table, I noticed a few pieces of clothing on top of her dresser. When I opened the top drawer to put them away, I found stacks and stacks of letters I had written her over the past several years. They were assembled in neat little rows. I decided to take them too.

Before we boarded our flight to Regina, I made sure that this precious cargo was zipped tightly inside a special carry-on bag that didn't leave my sight.

When we got back to Moose Jaw, my emotions were raw. I didn't feel like being around anyone. I didn't want to go for coffee with my close friends, even though by making the offer they were trying to be kind. All I wanted to do was put on my pyjamas and go to bed.

This lasted for a couple of days before I realized that life must go on.

I found solace in just being alone and reliving the precious memories I had of my mom. There were days when guilt consumed me because I hadn't been there when she died. According to Jean, she'd had a heart attack and didn't suffer.

After having a good talk with myself, I was able to let go of the guilt. I had been there for my mom while she was alive, and that's what mattered.

When my brother had died, I'd been nagged by two questions: had David known I loved him, and was he in heaven with God? These same questions were on my mind about my mom. Because I was able to answer an unequivocal yes to both, I felt peace and a deep sense of relief.

The next morning, I looked for any distraction, any reason not to start the household chores. I noticed my Bible on the kitchen table and seemed drawn to it more than usual. Opening it randomly, I read from John 16:

> In very truth I tell you, you will weep and mourn…
> But though you will be plunged in grief, your grief
> will be turned to joy… for the moment you are
> sad at heart; but I shall see you again, and then you
> will be joyful, and no one shall rob you of your joy.
> (John 16:20, 22)

Even though Jesus was speaking to His disciples, the message seemed to be meant especially for me. I had read this scripture countless times before, but its impact on me that day was profound. God's Word never disappoints. It's like manna from heaven. It satisfies our soul, giving us peace and comfort. Having just buried my mom days earlier, I certainly felt plunged into grief and sad at heart. It didn't seem plausible for my grief to be turned to joy.

As I reflected on that timely scripture, the words seemed to lull me into peacefulness, even though the void in my life from losing my mom penetrated deeply. I knew that the next time our phone rang, it wouldn't be her calling. And yet, like so many others facing loss, I thought about what a gift it would be if only I could hear from her one more time.

Then I watched as the letter-carrier delivered some items to our mailbox. I opened the front door to retrieve the mail and carry it inside to the kitchen table.

I'm glad I was sitting down as I went through it, or I'm sure I would have fainted and fallen onto the floor. I didn't have a problem with my eyesight, but I couldn't believe what I was seeing.

I picked up a letter. I would have recognized that handwriting anywhere.

It was a letter from my mom!

I opened the envelope carefully, like it was the most important document in the world, as if it was from royalty. And of course, to me it was.

Putting the envelope aside, I read the card my mom had written to me, dated June 15, 1994, just three days before her death. It was filled with her usual warm, loving sentiments and cheerful wishes. In addition to the card, I found a tiny jewellery box with a note attached: "Hi, my beautiful daughter. Whatever's in this box, it's all yours. All my love, always, Mom xo."

When I opened the box, inside were two rings—her gold wedding band and the family ring we had bought her many years before.

Holding her two rings in my hand, my grief was turned to joy. The tears streaming down my face at that moment were happy, tears of thankfulness that God works in such mysterious ways. His timing is perfect.

Getting my mom's card in the mail that day was like getting a love letter from heaven. I'll never know why my mom decided to mail her rings; we had never talked about it before. From time to time, I've wondered if she had a premonition. I do know that since becoming a Christian, she had depended on God's daily guidance to direct her path and light her way.

Since receiving that letter, its contents have found a new home in the top drawer of my dresser. Her rings still sit in the little box I found them in. On my mom's birthday and at Christmas, I take them out and hold them close to my heart, to remind myself that a mother's love never dies.

I believe that my mom has seen Jesus face to face. There is no need for prosthetics in heaven. Her body has been made whole. I'm sure she is dancing with the angels!

CHAPTER FOURTEEN

A LONG-AWAITED HEALING

Experiencing loss is part of everyone's journey. That can include the loss of a loved one, a family pet, our health, our home, or a job. And when we see our health deteriorating with no hope of improvement, that is cause for concern.

Even though I had given my attention to my parents' health situations, long before this I had privately been dealing with a medical issue of my own. Around the same time we had moved to Neville after John's ordination, I had started to notice my voice often becoming hoarse. I had frequent attacks of laryngitis. My throat was painful at times, a detrimental situation for a singer.

When I could no longer speak without extreme pain, I resorted to writing everything on a piece of paper. I had no voice. This is when we began making pilgrimages to doctors in Saskatchewan and Toronto. After each appointment, I was given yet another prescription for antibiotics, none of which helped.

This continued sporadically for a few years, until we moved to Moose Jaw, where John had accepted a new call to ministry. We had such excitement over meeting our new church family. We knew there would be all kinds of events planned to welcome the new pastor, his wife, and their young son.

Since my voice problems seemed to persist and relent at random times, I managed to participate in church activities at a comfortable level. Because music was a lifelong passion of mine, I couldn't resist joining the choir, occasionally taking part in special duets or trios and singing on the worship team.

For the next several years, I found myself not only taking part in Bible studies but also leading faith-based healing and prayer groups, one of which I called, "Where Are You on Your Journey of Faith?" It was a challenge, since I never knew when I would have a voice to sing, to lead, or to pray. Consequently, it was difficult for me to make firm commitments, and this was naturally followed by depression.

By this time, the problem had lasted more than fifteen years and there was no way of knowing if I would ever get my voice back or be able to sing with any amount of strength again. At times I felt broken, like a bird without wings.

I was reminded of the Apostle Paul and the thorn in his flesh, which he asked the Lord to take away. But God's answer was different than expected: *"My grace is sufficient for you, for my power is made perfect in weakness"* (2 Corinthians 12:9, NIV).

So I surrendered. "God, give me the strength to be weak," I prayed.

Looking ahead to the upcoming weekend, John and I had made plans, along with other members of our congregation, to attend a conference in Swift Current about the well-known Alpha course. Before we left on Friday, I knew I would need to make some time for prayer.

I found myself standing in our kitchen looking out a north-facing window into our backyard. Many a prayer had been said from that window and many a prayer had been answered.

Standing there, I unloaded my lamentations on God. I was so despondent and depressed, crying out to God from the depths of my soul and telling Him that I didn't think I could go on if I couldn't sing.

"I need You to heal me *this weekend*," I said to Him.

It was less than a two-hour drive to Swift Current and the conference agenda on Friday night was light. Time had been set aside for registration and dinner, followed by some social activities. There were no keynote speakers until Saturday.

After breakfast the next morning, we looked forward to learning more about the Alpha course to see if it would be a good fit for our congregation. As we entered the sanctuary, the worship team was singing the most uplifting songs. John and I slid into a pew and felt blessed by the infectious music. We joined with others, beginning to raise our voices in praise.

There was only one problem; I had no voice. As I tried to join the chorus of excited worshippers, all I felt was a painful hoarseness in my throat. The music was so refreshing and powerful, but I couldn't take part.

I excused myself and told John I would be in the lobby for a while.

I watched as people walked around, having coffee and chatting with each other. I just stood there feeling very much alone, more depressed than ever.

Within a couple of minutes, a woman approached me and asked me if I needed prayer.

"I sure do," I replied emphatically.

She escorted me to the prayer room where another woman was sitting, quietly waiting. The first woman introduced herself as Mary, and the second said that her name was Carol.

"That's my name too," I said.

I immediately felt comfortable with these soft-spoken, compassionate, genuinely interested women as I explained the problem. I focused entirely on my voice and felt no need to share about anything else.

With Carol on my left and Mary on my right, they offered an opening prayer as we bowed our heads. The prayer was followed by a few minutes of silence, during which I felt completely at ease. At least these women were willing to listen and pray; it was the perfect prescription for me, so much more helpful than all the useless pills I had accumulated from doctors for more than fifteen years.

"God has shown me the troubled childhood you had and all the violence in your life," Carol said after a while. "He has revealed to me that you were estranged from your alcoholic father. He has shown me that you ran away from home when you were very young and that you had many obstacles to overcome."

I was dumbfounded. I hadn't mentioned anything to them about my childhood, and yet Carol knew some very personal facts about my life. The only explanation I could see was that God had given her a word of knowledge to minister to me more effectively.

> One man, through the Spirit, has the gift of wise speech, while another, by the power of the same Spirit, can put the deepest knowledge into words. (1 Corinthians 12:8)

Then Carol told me something even more amazing. The problem I was having wasn't physical, it was spiritual. She explained that my lack of a loving father figure in my life had presented challenges even before I'd become a Christian. Because I hadn't felt acceptance from my own dad, I had only barely been able to conceive of being accepted by God, my heavenly Father.

I realized then and there that my dad had never made me feel like I was good enough for anything, and therefore I had expected the same ridicule from God. That kind of relationship is based on fear, not faith. For many years, it had been hard for me to relate to God's unconditional love, to fully embrace and receive it.

After I became a Christian, I passionately shared about Jesus and the Holy Spirit. Whether intended or not, I usually neglected to mention God. I'm sure this was because I had undergone such a powerful and dramatic experience of Jesus and the Holy Spirit.

But sitting there with Carol and Mary, examining my journey of faith, I openly acknowledged that everything Carol had revealed was true.

Regardless of whether I would be healed or not, Carol suggested that I needed to embrace the fatherhood of God in a more intentional manner. To have a healthy and mature faith, I needed to acknowledge God as my heavenly Father as much as I acknowledged Jesus and the Holy Spirit.

I may not have understood, theologically, the crossroads at which I found myself. All I knew was that the doctors and specialists had failed me; I had only gotten sicker. When I reflected on Carol's explanation, I found that it made sense. I recalled the words of the Apostle Paul again: *"I was given a sharp physical pain which came as Satan's messenger to bruise me..."* (2 Corinthians 12:7).

That's when I wondered whether the enemy had played a part in my illness—and if so, how much. I wasn't sure.

My thoughts briefly flashed back to the night when I had first walked forward to receive Jesus. I had promised God I would trust Him in everything. I knew it was now time for me to honour that commitment.

Carol and Mary wanted to pray specifically for my healing, so they each gently placed one hand on my shoulders. As we sat there together, they offered the most beautiful, heartfelt prayers. It was hard not to become emotional. Tears streamed down my face, as they often did for one reason or another.

When they finished praying, we all stood up and hugged each other. More than two hours had elapsed and we had indeed become friends in Christ.

Before I left the room, Carol smiled and said, "I believe you have received your healing." She also reminded me that when I returned home, I needed to include God in my prayers, in my praise, and in everything.

> Trust in the Lord with all your heart, and lean
> not on your own understanding; in all your ways
> acknowledge Him, and He shall direct your paths.
> (Proverbs 3:5–6, NKJV)

The conference ended on Sunday morning after the church service. Although I didn't feel any different physically and my voice was still missing in action, I continued to claim my healing and trusted God for it. I never doubted.

I knew that God had to have played a huge part in my prayer time with Carol and Mary. Running into them had been no coincidence. I believe that Carol had been guided by the Holy Spirit to approach me in the lobby. And it certainly hadn't been by chance that Carol had known so many intimate, specific facts about my childhood. God had given her a word of knowledge so she could minister to me as He directed.

All these circumstances had needed to be woven together perfectly, leading me to believe that God had healed my voice. I could see no other reason why He would intervene and direct this entire set of circumstances.

John and I got back from Swift Current ready to face a brand-new week. He went to work the next morning—and as soon as he drove out of the driveway, I sat at the kitchen table and said a prayer, asking God to forgive me for having excluded Him in my journey of faith all these years. I needed His forgiveness before I could move forward.

I listened to as many worship songs as I could find, exalting God, our heavenly Father. At times I found myself lifting my hands in praise or kneeling in prayer. This signified a turning point, a new chapter in my relationship with God. My heart erupted in praise and gratitude overflowed from within me. I knew I had been healed, and soon it would be clear that I had my voice back.

As I continued to put my trust in God, my pain diminished with each new day. Soon I could speak with ease. I began to wonder what other plans God had for me.

That was more than twenty-six years ago, and the problem has never returned. My voice has never been stronger; just ask my husband. Praise God!

BECAUSE OF YOU[4]

Because of You, there's a bright tomorrow and I realize the
blessings of each day.
Because of You, joy can come from sorrow and in Your love I've
found a better way.
Because of You.
I could scale the highest mountain to reach the tallest peak,
Then I'd kneel in prayer to give thanks from my heart.
To know I've finally found You and that I had the will to seek
And believe Your love was there right from the start.

Because of You, life has deeper meaning and this journey that I'm
on will see me through.
Because of You, I find my heart is dreaming of all that I've
become since I met You.
Because of You.
I could sail the deepest ocean to ride the tallest wave,
Then be showered by the magic of the sea.
To remind me of the memories and the blessings that I have
In the love that deeply flows from You to me.

A love so strong, my life's a song
Because of You, because of You.

---

[4] I wrote this song to share how much more meaningful, blessed, and full of joy life can
become when God guides our paths.

CHAPTER FIFTEEN
WHEN THE HOLY SPIRIT SPEAKS

Decades had passed since I first received Jesus as my Saviour and Lord, yet it felt like I had experienced more than a lifetime of incredible revelations from God.

From the night I committed my life to Christ, that dramatic first encounter formed the foundation for my journey of faith. I'd never asked for drama or anything supernatural. I hadn't needed to fall in the Spirit, and I hadn't expected visions of light or of speaking in tongues.

Of course, if I had been more familiar with scripture, I would have known that this was Basic Christianity 101. These manifestations are nothing new. God cannot change His supernatural nature just to fit our perception of who He is.

After receiving Jesus, I thought I would simply fade into the background for the rest of my life and read my Bible in peace and serenity. But how do we become the hands and feet of Christ by just sitting idle? That isn't what Jesus looked for when choosing disciples. Not then. Not now.

God can use us all to impact other people's lives. We don't need to wish we were someone else. We don't need to covet other people's spiritual gifts, since they would be a bad fit for us and wouldn't work in our lives anyway. We may not all need to be theologians or biblical scholars, but we do need to have a childlike faith and the simple trust to follow God and fulfill His purpose for our lives. That doesn't mean our faith lacks depth or is superficial. It means we know that God's in charge. He leads, we follow. He leads, we surrender. He leads, we obey. He leads, we pray. He leads.

Jesus tells us, *"My own sheep listen to my voice; I know them and they follow me"* (John 10:27). But we're only able to recognize the voice of Jesus when we're in relationship with Him. We cannot recognize the voice of a stranger; it's impossible because we don't know anything about a stranger. And so it is with the Holy Spirit. We need to be in fellowship with Him through His relationship with us as our Advocate, Comforter, Teacher, and Guide.

God refines and transforms us into a new creation, and as that refining process continues we learn to recognize Him speaking to us in different ways. This often happens through scripture, but it can also happen through conversations with other Christians, sermons, songs, movies, or books. God is not limited in how He chooses to get our attention.

But sometimes we're not looking in the right places. Sometimes we're not listening.

As I matured in my faith, I became very sensitive to the Holy Spirit and His leading. My ears perk up at any mention of the Holy Spirit in a sermon and I listen even more intently. My relationship with Him is deepening, causing me to recognize when He's prompting me to action—mostly, to pray.

Such was my experience one night when Josh and his friend Paul were returning from their university in Regina.

It was a Monday, which meant Josh would arrive home later than usual, somewhere around 7:00 p.m., because his classes went longer. I was in the habit of taking his food out of the fridge, setting it on the kitchen counter, and popping his plate in the microwave when I heard his car pull into the driveway.

I'd had an especially hectic day. Exhausted, I leaned back in my easy chair and drifted off to sleep without any effort while waiting for Josh.

I probably could have slept a lot longer, but around 7:20 p.m. I was abruptly awakened. I sat straight up, my eyes wide open as a sense of impending dread came over me. At that precise moment, I felt an overwhelming urge to pray for Josh's protection and safety. I had experienced this prodding in other situations before and I knew it was a prompting of the Holy Spirit. The reason for me to earnestly pray wasn't disclosed to me, but that wasn't important. The Holy Spirit is our Teacher and our classroom is life. I had learned that when the Spirit of God prompts us to pray, obedience is the only acceptable response.

I bowed my head and fervently prayed. Whenever I pray for a person's protection and safety, besides calling upon God to intervene, I always ask Him to send His army of angels to surround them. When Josh is driving on the highway or taking a flight somewhere, much of my time is spent in prayer until I know he is safe.

But this Monday night was more unsettling than I could have imagined.

Just before 8:00 p.m., with my head still bowed in prayer, I heard a car pull into the driveway. Someone unlocked the back door, near the kitchen.

As I walked to the door, I saw Josh standing there. I was relieved but still shaking. With my stomach still in knots, I told him that he looked as white as a sheet.

All he said to me was "That's because I almost died tonight."

They had left the university around the usual time. But when they were more than halfway home, they noticed the lights of an oncoming vehicle getting brighter and brighter, almost blinding them. Josh was driving, and he and Paul tried to figure out exactly what was happening. After a while, they realized that an old pickup truck was heading directly towards them. It was a divided highway but the truck driver was going the wrong way.

Right before the impending accident, Josh swerved out of the way and drove onto the shoulder, coming to a standstill.

Hardly believing what had just transpired, he and Paul sat there collecting their thoughts. They talked about what could have happened if Josh hadn't reacted in such a timely manner. I have no doubt that the Holy Spirit, our Advocate, had intervened.

As I listened to Josh relive the incident, I understood why the Holy Spirit had wakened me from sleep and implored me to pray. If I hadn't had a personal relationship with God's Spirit, I could have easily ignored His prompting.

God is mysterious. We can't even begin to understand at times how His Spirit works. The closest glimpse we have is in the scriptures. I believe that each time the Holy Spirit has summoned me to pray, that prayer has somehow greatly impacted the outcome, only because I was compliant to His leading. It has far less to do with me, and much more to do with His power to intervene.

If praying doesn't make any difference, why would the Holy Spirit instruct us to do so? And yet we can hardly take credit for being obedient, something God expects a devoted follower of Christ to be. God alone deserves the praise and glory! I simply prayed.

I'm reminded of a similar situation when prayer also made a difference. It was 2000 and John had been wanting to travel to the Holy Land for many years. He and Gord, a good friend, had signed up for a two-week guided tour. Once they arrived in Tel Aviv, John phoned to let me know they had landed safely, to put me at ease. Considering the time difference, we agreed that he would try to phone me every few days.

For the first week of his trip, John managed to stay in touch well, working around the tour group's busy schedule. When we talked, I mentioned that it might be slightly hard to reach me the following Sunday, though, because Josh and I would be at church. So he offered to phone again on Monday afternoon.

When Sunday arrived, as usual it was the highlight of our week. The service started and everything seemed fine.

But partway through the sermon, my thoughts turned to John and I discerned that something was wrong. Throughout the rest of the service, this feeling of peril only grew stronger.

Since becoming a Christian, I had received many previous promptings from the Holy Spirit to pray, so I recognized His petitioning now.

As soon as the service ended, I summoned two of my closest friends with whom I had prayed before, and explained to them that I felt we needed to pray for John. Everyone else had left the sanctuary and we approached the pulpit. There, we knelt as I prayed for John's protection and safety. My friends then offered their own prayers.

I could hardly wait for John's phone call Monday. I sensed that he, and perhaps the tour group, may be facing a precarious situation. Prayer was the only remedy.

For the next several hours, time seemed to stand still. I tried to keep busy and not worry, trusting that our prayers of intercession had accomplished their purpose.

I had just finished putting away the last of the lunch dishes when the phone rang; it was John. What a blessing to hear his voice! I breathed a sigh of relief.

He began to tell me all about the tour and recent events. Then he paused.

"You won't believe what happened today," he said.

"Oh, I think I will."

A special trip had been scheduled that everyone had been anticipating. The tour group had boarded a bus and left Petra, an ancient archaeological ruin in southern Jordan, and continued along the King's Highway heading north.

They stopped at Mount Nebo in Israel. After the tour guide highlighted several historic facts, their bus left again and headed down the mountain.

Only minutes later, the bus driver realized there was something malfunctioning with the bus but managed to guide it safely into a pullout.

When the bus coasted to a stop, the driver explained that the brakes had failed and it was impossible to proceed. As soon as all the passengers had disembarked, they heard a loud, menacing hiss. Before too long, another bus arrived to take them back to their hotel.

When the Holy Land tour was over, John and the rest of the group returned to Regina on an uneventful flight. Less than an hour after that, I was greeting him at our front door, helping him bring in his luggage.

After he relaxed later that night, he showed me some of the treasures he had brought back. Then we looked at pictures and postcards he had purchased. When he showed me a picture of Mount Nebo and recalled the perilous situation they'd faced, I thought it was the perfect time to tell him about how I had felt that Sunday in church.

As we traced the timing of our prayer to the tour group's visit to Mount Nebo, we were able to deduce that the two events had occurred within hours of each other. Recalling that part of the tour, John admitted how hazardous the situation was and how fortunate they were not to have perished.

When I reminisce about the incredible direction my journey of faith has taken, it's clear that the Holy Spirit has had a hand, literally, in guiding my path. I don't pretend to understand. For me, there is no rhyme or reason to help me comprehend the mystery of His nature.

But how I love Him! He is the Gift that keeps on giving. When He makes a promise, He never disappoints. He never lets us down. He keeps His Word.

CHAPTER SIXTEEN

WE DON'T NEED TO SWING FROM THE CHANDELIERS, BUT...

Imagine that some good friends of yours are taking a trip and they promise to bring back a gift for you. Upon their return, they hand you the gift but you refuse to take it. Can you picture how your friends would feel? Probably disappointed, perplexed, sad, disheartened, and rejected, among other things.

In God's Word, He promises to bless us with an abundant life and many spiritual endowments, including the gift of the Holy Spirit. I can only imagine how God must feel when we refuse to receive that gift, especially when Jesus asked His Father to send it.

Throughout my past forty years as a Christian, I have witnessed many miraculous instances of God, through His Spirit, weaving His purpose and power together in people's lives. I marvel at the things I have seen and am truly humbled to have played a small part in some of them.

But I have also often witnessed the Holy Spirit being rejected and ignored as part of the Trinity. This saddens me more than I can say and I'm sure it must grieve God's heart.

I didn't plan on writing this chapter, but after prayerful consideration I have decided to share some of my relevant observations. These are not criticisms. I'm sure as devoted Christians we're all trying to reach others for Christ in the best way we know how. But that's the point: the best way we know how may not be enough.

We may be trying to witness and minister to others in our own strength and power. But if we could effectively carry out that mission by ourselves, there would have been no need for Jesus to ask His Father to send the Holy Spirit.

We may pride ourselves on having excellent communication skills, being a graduate of a public relations program, or having empathy to reach others for Christ. But even with all these attributes, we are ill-equipped to produce the permanent transformation only God can deliver. There is no substitute for the spiritual gifts God has provided through the Holy Spirit, as outlined in scripture:

> There are varieties of gifts, but the same Spirit.
> There are varieties of service, but the same Lord.
> There are many forms of work, but all of them, in
> all men, are the work of the same God. In each of
> us the Spirit is manifested in one particular way,
> for some useful purpose. (1 Corinthians 12:4–7)

Before we can desire to know the Holy Spirit, we must realize that He exists. After talking to people for decades, even those who have attended church most of their lives, I've noticed an honest uncertainty about the purpose of the Holy Spirit and the role He has been designated to play in our faith. I've heard Him referred to as "it" and a "force," but He is neither. He is a Person and can become just as real to us as God the Father and Jesus the Son.

For that to happen, though, we need to know the scriptures and have the courage to be obedient to their instruction. As we glean more of an understanding of who the Holy Spirit is, hopefully we can prayerfully embrace and receive God's promised gift in our lives.

If we insist on keeping a huge distance between us and the Holy Spirit, how can we ever expect to experience the fullness of God? Is reading and studying about the Holy Spirit enough to ensure that we possess a contagious, dynamic faith?

I'm reminded of what Jesus says:

> You study the scriptures diligently, supposing that in having them you have eternal life; yet, although their testimony points to me, you refuse to come to me for that life. (John 5:39–40)

I think it may be beneficial to consider some specific examples. Is it enough to sit back and spectate, or must we gain our own experience?

Think of a young man who wants to get his driver's licence. He enrolls in a driver training course. The instructor, however, never actually lets the student sit behind the wheel. As the weeks pass, the young man remains a passenger and is never offered an opportunity to start the car. The student reads and studies the driver's manual yet remains unfamiliar with what it feels like to drive.

Would he feel more comfortable, more confident, if he were encouraged to put the keys in the ignition and start driving?

Here's another example. Consider the case of a young wife who wants to know what it feels like to have a baby. In her desire to understand, she reads pamphlets and medical journals about how her body will change. She watches a video of new mothers exclaiming about the joy of feeling their baby move for the first time. Her friends even share how they felt when they gave birth.

The young woman continues to read volumes of material on childbirth, but she can only imagine what it feels like to carry a baby for nine months. If she became pregnant and had a baby, would this personal experience be more rewarding?

Again, there is a difference between being a passive observer and an active participant.

This reminds me of a women's Bible study I took part in when John and I lived in Kitchener. The six-week video presentation on the Holy Spirit was in-depth, covering the spiritual gifts, prayer, and the laying on of hands.

After each video, the group was given the chance to make comments and ask questions. Even though many of us in the discussion were at different places in our faith, it was clear that prayer was important to everyone. Some had never been prayed for with the laying on of hands and others had.

Soon the six weeks were over, but many people's passion to know the Holy Spirit more intimately was just beginning. As the last session concluded, some of the women stood waiting as though they wanted to be prayed for, just as I had been prayed for at the Alpha conference. But the church lights were turned off, the doors were locked, and the opportunity to pray for each other was never given.

I often wonder what might have happened if we had prayed for each other. How might those prayers have empowered people's relationship with God? And how might those prayers have been answered?

There may be occasions when we neglect to take time to wait upon the Holy Spirit. But when we fail to include Him, something's missing. Or more correctly, Someone's missing. It would be like taking part in a communion service, reciting all the liturgy, but never actually being invited to receive the bread and wine. In such a case, we would be left scratching our heads and wondering, *Isn't there more?*

God wants our faith to mature. At times, we are able to take baby steps in our journey to know Him better. But somewhere along the way those steps need to bring us into a deeper relationship with God through the Holy Spirit. That requires interaction and fellowship.

Now a word about prayer. I have prayed for people as they sat across from me at my dining room table. And I have prayed for people as I held their hand, or as I placed my hand on their shoulder, or on their forehead, as I led them to receive Jesus. There is no comparison.

When we touch other people, praying in the name of Jesus, there is a transfer of God's power to them—through us. It is undeniable. As I've said before, we are the hands and feet of Christ, and we are only vessels, allowing God's power to flow through us. Is this the only way in which God can use us, respond to our prayers, or fill us with the Holy Spirit? No. But God is pleased when the body of Christ ministers to each other effectively.

By studying the scriptures, it seems clear that the disciples modelled what they saw Jesus do. They watched and learned as Jesus reached out and prayed for others, not at arm's length but through the power of touch. And we can also include touch as part of our outreach and ministry. Surrendering to the Holy Spirit and using His gifts doesn't exalt ourselves; it builds up the body of Christ.

When I reflect on my experience at the Alpha conference, I realize that it made a significant difference when Carol revealed those facts about my childhood. The Holy Spirit convinced me that God was surely present in that prayer room, and I was supposed to be there.

Sadly, there seems to be a reluctance for churches to fully embrace and teach congregations about who the Holy Spirit is and help nurture the spiritual gifts He intends for our use. Perhaps members of the clergy fear not being fully in control, and that is understandable. But we're not supposed to be in control. Jesus invites us to receive the *full* Gospel, not two-thirds of it. Jesus told His disciples that He didn't want to leave them as orphans, so He asked His Father to send them a Helper, the Holy Spirit.

Do our congregations need a Helper today? Are our churches half-full or half-empty? Have some churches closed their doors permanently?

Think of how entire ministries could be transformed by a power greater than our own. It just means surrendering to a power from on high—our Advocate, Comforter, Teacher, and Guide. When you look at your own life, or the life of the church you attend, do you want to dare to dream the dreams God has for you? The Bible teaches that God has poured out the Holy Spirit for us all to drink. That doesn't mean He has only provided a tiny trickle of the Spirit for us to carefully ration among ourselves. God is a generous giver, and He offers His Spirit in abundance.

And yet as we dip our toes into the water of the Spirit's presence, wading deeper into that overflowing stream, we need to exercise a healthy caution. Scripture teaches that we serve a God of order, not chaos. He doesn't approve of a circus environment under the guise of His holy name. I have witnessed some bizarre activities in the name of religion. I'm thankful that the Holy Spirit has given me the gift of discernment to recognize the deception I've seen at certain so-called "Christian" events.

One such occasion happened many years ago when a religious group from Toronto advertised a weekend event in Regina. I decided to attend along with some close Christian friends. The weekend began innocently enough, with special praise music on

Friday night. But as the group's leaders shared their message on Saturday, I saw red flags everywhere.

After the speakers finished, a time of "ministry" followed, with everyone invited forward to receive prayer. While that continued, some stood on their hands and knees, like animals, which was strange enough. But when they started barking like dogs, I knew we were in the wrong place. At the same time, others were laughing uncontrollably, which apparently can continue for hours. The leaders of the gathering referred to this as holy laughter. I became even more perplexed when members of the Toronto group walked through the crowd encouraging others to imitate this unconventional practice.

I don't pretend to know my Bible from cover to cover, but I was familiar enough to realize that this bizarre behaviour isn't included in any scripture I've ever read. My friends and I decided that this strange conduct didn't glorify God in any way. As soon as we located an exit, we left the building.

When we reached the highway, the sign to Moose Jaw never looked so inviting.

The whole point of sharing this is to illustrate the importance of having a deep, authentic relationship with the Holy Spirit. We need to be confident enough in our faith, and strong enough in our convictions, to know that when something doesn't feel right, it's probably not. When we learn to trust the Holy Spirit's leading, we should feel peace, not anxiety or distress.

No, we don't need to swing from the chandeliers, but we also don't need to roll in the aisles or bark like dogs. With the gift of discernment given to us by the Holy Spirit, we can easily recognize the true nature of God and what is acceptable to Him. And to us.

My sincere prayer is for us all to deepen our relationship with our heavenly Father, Jesus, and the Holy Spirit. An infinite number of Bible passages encourage us to draw closer to God through our openness to the Holy Spirit. Here is one of my favourites:

> "Repent," said Peter, "repent and be baptized, every one of you, in the name of Jesus the Messiah for the forgiveness of your sins; and you will receive the gift of the Holy Spirit. For the promise is to you, and to your children, and to all who are far away, everyone whom the Lord our God may call." (Acts 2:38–39)

CHAPTER SEVENTEEN

THE SOUND OF MUSIC

Despite the roller coaster turns my life had taken as a child, God had always given me a song to sing. I forever had a song in my heart and a new one to write.

Around the time I ran away from home, I started to write poems and songs whenever I could. Because my self-esteem was so low and my self-image poor, even a seasoned sleuth would rarely have been able to catch me talking to anyone. Having been rejected by my dad, I wasn't willing to risk taking the chance of making many friends. Talking was scary. Writing wasn't.

I wanted to express my innermost feelings somehow, so putting pen to paper seemed a less vulnerable method. Throughout high school and college, I accumulated a rather large collection of writing. It didn't matter to me that no one else would see it. In fact, I knew I was probably the only person who would ever read my poetry or listen to my songs.

In 2001, God gave me the inspiration to write several new songs, and before too long I had a collection of eight. I knew He must have given me this music for a reason, and after I prayed about it the answer came to me: I was supposed to make a CD. I didn't know how that was going to happen, I just trusted that God was going to bring this project to fruition.

And so my first album became a reality. To honour God and thank Him for so many blessings in my life, I called it *You Are the Reason*. In my role as music director, I invited people from the church and community to take part and was excited to have more than fifty enthusiastic singers comprise the choir. Our goal was to practice and memorize the music for nearly three months and then present it in church.

Until this point, I had sung and recorded the songs on a tape recorder. Because I didn't read or write music, the next challenge was figuring out how to create the actual sheets of music.

I didn't have to look any further than my own address. Not only was Josh a trained tenor, but he had taken piano lessons since the age of five. Music was as much a part of his life as mine.

It was going to be a rather primitive process to transform my songs into actual written music, but we had no other option. Being a devoted, good-natured son, Josh took on the tedious task of transposing the songs into sheet music so the choir could learn them.

The Sunday morning soon arrived when we would present our music to the congregation. As I directed the choir and listened to them weave their voices together, I couldn't have been prouder of them for all their hard work and extra hours of practice. I was truly humbled to be part of this journey and labour of love.

Even more emotional for me was the opportunity to share this ministry of music with my son. Not only was the music a gift from God, but so was Josh.

As the months passed, my faith seemed to burn even brighter for God. Whether I was meeting friends for coffee, praying for someone with a specific need, or leading someone to receive Jesus, a deep sense of gratitude flowed within me.

Hardly able to contain my praise and thankfulness, I decided to channel this passion into a second album. In 2002, God inspired me to write twelve new songs for my second collection, called *You Gotta Have Faith!* In those recordings, more than sixty people joined their voices to lift their praise to God! The process was similar this time around, the biggest change being that we recorded the music live in church! Even the local media attended our presentation that Sunday.

Just as I had done before, I invited anyone who loved music to become part of this endeavour. There were no auditions, no need to read music, no previous singing experience required. All that was necessary was a genuine love of God and a desire to reflect it through song. I knew the disappointment of being left out of things, or not feeling good enough, which is why I included everyone.

Around the same time our music practices began, John and I had some new carpet installed at home. When the manager of the carpet store, Earl, came to our house to finalize the floor measurements, I asked him if he liked to sing. He ended up committing himself to the whole project, showing up for every practice and revealing his beautiful tenor voice.

I realized we weren't going to be nominated for a Juno award. That was never the goal. But we were sure going to make a joyful noise!

Two of the songs on my second album have special significance. The first, "The Gift You Are," is a tribute to Josh. It conveys a mother's love for her son. The other, "Holy Are You, Lord," is unique because of how it came about. Let me explain.

I had only one song left to write. As I washed dishes one night, it occurred to me that I wanted to write a song with as few lyrics as possible. The words "Holy Are You, Lord" popped into my mind along with the melody. That's when I decided to use only those four words in the whole song.

My tape recorder was downstairs, so I went down, pressed record, and sang the song. No sooner had I returned to continue washing dishes than another melody, with the same words, came to my mind. I went downstairs and recorded it directly after the first melody.

When I returned upstairs, the process happened all over again. At that point, I had sung these simple lyrics to three completely different melodies. I wondered whether I might save myself a trip and just wait downstairs for the fourth part of the song to arrive!

While standing there, I decided how the choir would present the song: a soloist would sing the first melody, a different soloist would sing the second, and another soloist would sing the third. Then the whole choir would sing each part consecutively. That sounded simple enough.

But just before I went back upstairs, I began to get an impression from the Holy Spirit: after the choir had finished singing as I'd planned, there would be one addition. To end the song, I would divide the choir into three equal groups, with each one singing their melody with the others simultaneously.

As I've mentioned before, I don't read or write music, so I had no idea if this would work. What about the timing? And when all three parts were sung together, would they be in perfect harmony?

There was only one way for me to test this hypothesis.

When I played back the first melody on the tape recorder, I sang the second melody along with it. Then I played the second melody and sang the third melody. I continued to test the theory until I had sung all three melodies together. To my utter amazement, the timing and harmonies were perfect.

I wasn't only astonished; I didn't even see how this was humanly possible. You could have knocked me over with a feather. I was astounded that the Holy Spirit had imprinted this idea in my mind, not to mention that I had been able to understand it. He had intervened to create a much more powerful song than what I had originally written.

Later that week, I got together with Josh so he could arrange the music. Everything was going quite well until I offered the final suggestion of dividing the choir into three parts and have them sing the melodies together. He knew I didn't read music and looked at me like I was from Mars. But then he played all the parts together on the piano, and voila! It was powerful.

I can't take any credit for it. The Holy Spirit, in His role as Teacher and Guide, wrote and directed the entire song. I just had to follow His instruction.

After the album was recorded and produced, I was humbled to listen to the congregation's response following each song. I had chosen different soloists for specific songs and had asked them to give an introduction; it was meaningful to listen as they each related their testimonies.

When it was time for me to sing "The Gift You Are," I stood right beside Josh as he played the accompaniment. As the music started, I didn't feel like a soloist. I was just a mother singing about her son, such a precious gift. There could be no crying allowed for the live recording, and I somehow managed to get through it without any tears.

When our special presentation was over, I ended the recording with a prayer of thanks to God for the gift of music. Gathering with the choir members and deepening our bonds of friendship had been a bonus. Throughout the months of practice, I had made sure to emphasize that we weren't offering a performance but rather presenting a ministry. That's also how I felt about the songs that were played during our worship services.

Afterward I found myself preoccupied with how much I still missed my brother, David, and the many occasions we hadn't been able to celebrate together. I also asked myself what kind of legacy I was going to leave. Had I truly embraced the purpose God intended for me? Had I really touched the lives of others? Most importantly, I pondered the message I wanted to leave. When people look at my life, do they know that God is a huge part of it? Are they able to see the light of Jesus shining in me? And when I see Jesus face to face, will He say, *"Well done, good and faithful servant!"* (Matthew 25:21 NIV)?

With all these emotions welling up inside me, I knew I was about to write some new songs. In fact, in 2003 I wrote ten new songs, including two of which were especially meaningful. The song about my brother was entitled "For the Love of David" and the other was "Legacy," which also became the title of my third album.

As usual, the choir presented the music during a Sunday worship service. More than sixty faithful singers committed to the project. Immense gratitude filled my heart for having the incredible opportunity to share such personal feelings through the songs God inspired me to write. I was even more humbled to receive many kind and thoughtful cards thanking me for the music.

I then remembered that one of the songs on my first album had been entitled "The Praise Is for You." It was a tribute to God, praising Him alone for the gift of music.

Three of the cards I received were from women who had also lost a brother named David. Each of them personally shared how the song had helped to soothe their sorrow and bring some healing. This touched me deeply and I still find myself occasionally reading those cards and letters. I have kept them all these years.

Included in the notes were numerous thanks to Josh for his extraordinary keyboard accompaniment, solos, and harmony. His contagious spirit and ingenious creativity were evident and continue to shine in the many projects he has embraced.

As music director at Cornerstone Christian School in Moose Jaw, Josh's choirs have been blessed with exceptional opportunities. The concert choir was selected to perform in 2015 with the Canadian Tenors at Mosaic Place. And as director of the Moose Jaw Children's Choir, they accepted an invitation to sing at the United Nations in New York.

Though tempted, I'll refrain from listing Josh's numerous other career highlights. However, I would be remiss not to mention two personal accomplishments. The first is when he attended the University of Regina and was chosen to sing "Spinning Wheel," accompanied by jazz musician and trumpet player Lew Soloff of Blood, Sweat and Tears. The second is his recent original song, "When You Return," which can be found on YouTube.[5]

Without the gift of music, our lives would be far less rich. Music is a universal language that spans oceans to unite our hearts and souls. Even when people from different cultures otherwise remain strangers, music can transcend barriers to foster good will, love, and harmony. Creating and sharing music is an admiral legacy worth leaving.

<hr>

[5] Josh Carley, "When You Return," *YouTube*. Date of access: August 14, 2023 (https://www.youtube.com/watch?v=LfK6vku_Zao&ab_channel=VariousArtists-Topic).

THE GIFT YOU ARE

When I think of how my life was without you,
So many thoughts of hopelessness were on my mind.
I didn't have the faith I'd need to see me through.
Any rainbows the Lord sent I couldn't find.
Then one day I said a prayer to God above
And I asked Him for a miracle, just one.
And in no time He sent me a gift of love,
Something more to live for, a new son.

Chorus
The gift you are, the gift you are.
When my universe seemed empty,
You became the brightest star.
The gift you are, the gift you are.
Do you realize the gift you are?

I remember how I really felt back then.
I couldn't find a deeper purpose to live for.
No one knew my secret pain, I'd just pretend.
But deep inside I thought there must be more.
When my footsteps seemed to falter through and through,
Then I asked the Lord if He would carry me.
And He gave me strength so I could carry you.
Then He sent a ray of hope so I could see.

<u>Chorus</u>
The gift you are, the gift you are.
When my universe seemed empty,
You became the brightest star.
The gift you are, the gift you are.
Do you realize it's
Really no surprise
When I look into your eyes
I can see the gift you are?

CHAPTER EIGHTEEN
LEGACY

We are all going to leave a legacy of one kind or another. This legacy can be a gift to our children and grandchildren, more precious than silver or gold.

Besides love, the best thing we can leave our family is the gift of time. What really matters is how we spend our time while we're still here. The things we say to others are important, but it's what we do that will help ensure we pass along memories worth cherishing.

Whether we're in the prime of life or acquainted with our golden years, it's never too late to make a difference or start a new tradition. But I've met seniors who think there's nothing left to live for when they reach a certain birthday or a few strands of hair turn grey. That is a myth.

I'm reminded of a dear eighty-two-year-old widow named Shirley. She approached me after church one Sunday and told me something that broke my heart: "I've gone to church my whole life, but I don't know Jesus." She asked if I would come to her home and tell her about Him, so we arranged a time to do it a couple of days later.

I sat with Shirley at her kitchen table and read with her some of the scriptures I felt were most important. I also explained why I'd brought a beautiful framed picture of Jesus knocking on a door—something I bring, along with my Bible, anytime I lead someone to Jesus. To go along with the picture, I read the related verse in Revelation 3:20:

> Here I stand knocking at the door; if anyone hears
> my voice and opens the door, I will come in…

When Shirley felt ready, I clasped her hands in mine and led her in prayer to receive Jesus. Tears streamed down her face as she admitted how thankful she was to have taken this personal step of faith.

In the days and years that followed, she joined a home Bible study group in her neighbourhood. She contacted me months later to say that she told her grandchildren about her special prayer. Her legacy had just increased in value!

I had often seen Shirley at church but hadn't known her well. As I reflected on my prayer time with her, I wondered whether she had contemplated committing her life to Christ for years but just hadn't felt ready. Had she simply not been encouraged and taught about receiving Jesus? Hadn't she been given the opportunity through the decades? God help us if it was the latter.

The ministry of the church has an all-encompassing mandate that includes social activities, Bible studies, youth programs, community outreach, weddings, funerals, and everything in between. All of this is important. But I hope the heart of the church's mission never wavers from its focus on helping people receive and know Jesus.

Imagine going to church and after the worship service mentioning to someone that you want to commit your life to Christ. Consider if this was the response: "Oh, you'll have to wait. We can't find the pastor." Or maybe "You'll have to phone the office next week and make an appointment."

Hopefully there are a significant amount of trained people in any congregation who are confident enough to lead another person to receive Christ. We need to know how to do this. We need to know how to disciple others.

Years ago, when my mom expressed her desire to know Jesus, I clearly thought that God had chosen someone else to minister to her. But when the Holy Spirit directed me to read Romans 10:11–17, I no longer had any doubt that I was the person God had chosen to do the honours. It would have been foolish for me to keep denying what I knew to be true.

God doesn't expect us to carry out His work alone. He knows we are powerless to accomplish these seemingly formidable challenges on our own. Even Jesus knew that the disciples wouldn't be victorious in carrying out the purpose He had set before them. But He was certain, with the Holy Spirit as their Guide, that all things are possible.

In two thousand years, God's message hasn't changed.

We're all fellow travellers on a journey. No one wants to travel the distance by themselves, nor should anyone have to. As members of the body of Christ, we need to build one another up, not tear each other down. Praying with someone may seem like the smallest, most trivial gesture, but it may be the most impactful, profound act of kindness we can offer.

At times it may be hard to stop and help someone else when our own journey is proving to be so difficult. But there are lots of bends in the road, and sooner or later we may recognize that we don't have to keep going in the same direction. As we navigate the bumps along the way, we may need to change course.

Anything worth having, anything worth accomplishing, never seems to come easy. Maybe it's not supposed to. Maybe that has been God's intention all along, so that when we reach our goal and savour our success we can reflect on the integrity, determination, and perseverance we needed in order to capture the prize. When the journey is over and we reach our destination, hopefully we can acknowledge that we didn't do it alone. We can give God the glory for pushing and pulling us in the right direction when we needed it.

Jesus promised us many things, but He never said that our lives would be free of problems, heartache, pain, or suffering if we follow Him. Yet He did tell us that He'd be there to pick up the pieces when things fall apart. He wouldn't abandon us. He would send a Helper. I'm so thankful that Jesus meets us where we're at, carries us through the storms of life, and empowers us to rise above the challenges to be victorious!

Journeys can be daunting. We can either let the mountain stand in our way, blocking our view, or we can climb to the top, despite the struggles, and gain a whole new perspective. Even if you consider yourself an unlikely follower of Jesus, like me, you can have the most incredible journey of faith! Your pilgrimage may start with a wounded heart, but I pray that you will possess a healed spirit when you reach your destination.

That's truly a legacy worth living for.

THERE'S A MOUNTAIN[6]

There's a mountain that I'm climbing,
I'm afraid sometimes it gets in the way.
Life would be carefree and easy, Lord, if You'd take it away.

There's a journey that I'm taking,
finding answers that begin with myself.
Life might be much more appealing, Lord, if I was someone else.

To leave the world a richer, brighter place
And make a difference in the lives I see.
If only I could bless the human race
But, Lord, I'm only me.

There's a mountain that I'm climbing,
but my footsteps never get very far.
Will I understand these mountains, Lord,
when I reach where You are?

---

[6] I love gazing up at mountains. They reflect such grandeur and majesty. I wrote this song to represent what they mean to me. At times they've symbolized something that has stood in my way of pursuing a goal. I'm sure we've all had questions we hope to ask the Lord when we see Him. This is one of mine: why did I have so many mountains to climb along the way?

LEGACY

There's a world around us aching to be heard.
There's someone beside you needing a kind word.
Faith will guide our journey as we learn to give
Hope to generations; love will be the truth by which we live.

There's a dream within you waiting to be born.
There's a calm that follows after every storm.
Wars may rage around us, but our light will shine
Like a candle burning for a brighter future, yours and mine.

Where do we go from here to find the strength within,
To let go of the fear so hope can live again?
With faith we will go on to be all we can be,
Through us Your life will bring our greatest legacy.

There's a song of children echoing throughout,
Voices filled with laughter bringing hope, not doubt.
There's a God in heaven reaching out to you and me,
Giving us the courage to leave behind our greatest legacy!
To leave behind our greatest legacy!

ABOUT THE AUTHOR

Carol Carley is a graduate of the communication arts program at Canadore College in North Bay, Ontario. She also graduated from the journalism program at Conestoga College in Kitchener, Ontario.

Her career began as a communications assistant in public relations at Lutheran Life Insurance Society of Canada in Waterloo, Ontario where she worked for more than six years.

Her journalism training includes working for the Kitchener-Waterloo Record. She later became a reporter at the Stratford Beacon-Herald. She served as a reporter and lifestyles editor at the Moose Jaw Times-Herald for more than five years, where she also wrote a weekly column entitled "That's Life." While at the Times-Herald, she was nominated for the 1991 National Award of Excellence among peers for her in-depth research, content, and style of writing.

Her poetry has been published in Country Preacher's Notebook, 1990, by Joyce Sasse and The Warbler's Song, A New Collection of Canadian Poetry, 2014.

She has written original songs for three albums: *You Are the Reason* (2001), *You Gotta Have Faith* (2002), and *Legacy* (2003). She also directed a sixty-voice choir, which was featured on the CDs.

You can contact her at carolcarley@sasktel.net and on Facebook or Instagram.

www.ingramcontent.com/pod-product-compliance
Lightning Source LLC
Chambersburg PA
CBHW07202204026

42447CB00009B/1689